MATH PLAY

40 **Engaging Games for the Differentiated Classroom**

Eliza Sorte-Thomas

Crystal Springs **BOOKS**
SDE
A division of Staff Development for Educators

Crystal Springs Books
Peterborough, New Hampshire

Published by Crystal Springs Books
10 Sharon Road, PO Box 500
Peterborough, NH 03458
1-800-321-0401
www.SDE.com/crystalsprings

© 2015 Eliza Sorte-Thomas

Illustrations © 2015 Crystal Springs Books
Printed in the United States of America
18 17 16 15   2 3 4 5

ISBN: 978-1-935502-88-3
e-book ISBN: 978-1-935502-89-0

Library of Congress Cataloging-in-Publication Data

Sorte-Thomas, Eliza.

Math play : 40 engaging games for the differentiated classroom /
Eliza Sorte-Thomas.

    pages cm

ISBN 978-1-935502-88-3

    1. Games in mathematics education.   2. Mathematics—Study and

teaching—Activity programs.   I. Title.

    QA20.G35S67 2015

    372.7—dc23

                                        2014003982

This book is dedicated to all of the folks
(including my mom, Anne Sorte; my husband,
Jason Thomas; my best friends; my bonus daughters;
my SDE colleagues; my co-op colleagues;
Mrs. Burnham and my fourth-grade buddies;
and my numerous students, young and old)
who have taught me to be playful,
personally and professionally.

May this book allow teachers
the opportunity to be playful too,
in a mindful way, in their classrooms!

Contents

Introduction

Many times math games are pulled out at the end of the year as time fillers or are used only on Fridays as a break from the day-to-day routine of school. But math games are so much more.

Games are an essential component of math instruction, as well as a sanity saver that motivates students to achieve success. Games are good instructional practice as well as engaging applications of mathematical content. As a savvy teacher, you should always have games at your disposal as a strategy for actively involving students in math. I couldn't have survived a decade-plus in my own classroom without games; they are that important. Now, as director of a cooperative that supports education in multiple school districts and as a math consultant, I see how math games benefit students and teachers in classrooms everywhere I travel. Additionally, as a weekly volunteer in a fourth-grade classroom, I get to share in the fun, learning, and success of math games live and in person!

What makes games so important? Games can help meet the expectations set forth by the Common Core State Standards for Mathematics in an engaging and meaningful way. Games give students the chance to develop both competence and self-confidence with mathematics. Just as important, games allow a classroom teacher to differentiate math for the readiness levels of diverse learners.

Games also provide a home-school connection that is motivating and easy to encourage—unlike many traditional tasks. Nighttime battles around the kitchen table over completing 50 worksheet problems do not endear mathematics to anyone at home. But a game that parents or siblings can play with students supports learning and develops positive attitudes toward mathematics that can last a lifetime.

This book provides professional information about the process for planning and using games to meet a variety of learning needs, along with 40 ready-to-use games that require only minimal preparation. Yes, these are games—but they're also serious, worthwhile practice.

Have some serious fun!

—Eliza Sorte-Thomas

How to Use This Book

Games as Serious Fun

Games are fun, but they're also a serious tool for helping your students master and understand math. Part I of this book provides professional advice—from the pedagogical to the practical—on using games as part of your math instruction.

Games as an Instructional Strategy

Imagine a classroom that comes alive as students have the chance to experience a math lesson through the lens of a game. Students are mastering math facts, developing conceptual understanding, and applying mathematical practices, even as they are competing, collaborating, and having fun. Meanwhile, the teacher is gathering important data to help drive instruction.

Games are a valid and effective tool to use in everyday mathematical instruction, not just as a reward, time filler, or Friday afternoon treat. They are a purposeful choice made by the teacher to enhance instruction and place learning in the hands of students—sometimes as the lesson, sometimes as an intervention or extension, sometimes as homework, and sometimes as a way to keep all students meaningfully engaged while the teacher works with individuals.

All of this takes planning. For games to fulfill their potential as instructional tools, they must be thoroughly and thoughtfully connected to student outcomes. We can't just pull games from our files because they're fun. We must choose the right game for the right student at the right time. We need to first ask ourselves, "What do I want my students to be better at tomorrow?" and next ask, "Which game will help my students get there?" Then, when the class is playing a game we've chosen, we're ready to answer the question "Why are you playing this game today?" whether it's posed by a student, a parent, or an administrator.

Connecting Games to the Common Core

Ideally, students should know what math they're mastering while playing a game. How can they reach a target if they don't know what it is? Let students know exactly what the Common Core math standards say they should be learning. Make a poster of the CCSS clusters and standards within each domain for your class's grade level, or provide copies for students to keep in their notebooks. Refer to the standards as they learn new math skills and concepts.

Connecting to Clusters: As students learn a new game, challenge them to figure out which content cluster(s) the game addresses and to justify their answers. (You have this information in the CCSS box in the bottom corner of each game's right-hand page.) Acknowledge that some games address more than one cluster or even more than one domain. After students have played a game, have them write the game's name next to the content cluster on their copy of the CCSS standards, or use a sticky note to put it on the class poster. Students will see the connection between the games they're playing and the learning they're doing.

Connecting to Mathematical Practices: Explicitly connecting these games to the eight Mathematical Practices is another way to ensure that students understand what they gain when they play. Some games require perseverance, which is the essence of Mathematical Practice 1. Others make use of repeated reasoning (Practice 8), and still others ask students to use tools appropriately and strategically (Practice 5). As with the clusters, the practices supported by a game are listed in the CCSS box in the bottom corner of the right-hand page.

8 Math Play • Part I

Right Game, Right Time, Right Reason

When you're considering when to use games from this book, or even games of your own, you need to think about the amount of time it will take to teach and play the game, the materials required, and how long it will take to hand out those materials. You should also consider the complexity of the game, how long it will take to teach if this is the first time playing it, and the level of excitement it will generate. In my class, if we started class with a game like BACON (pages 44 to 45), it would get students all riled up. Bringing them back to focus on something else was a challenge, so I learned to save it for the end of the day, or right before lunch. Choosing the right games for a particular time of day was one of those things I learned over the years by trial and big error!

Games for Concrete–Pictorial–Abstract

When students are new to a concept, they need to move and manipulate concrete objects. For example, counting 7 seashells and then counting 3 more seashells shown in a concrete way that 7 plus 3 equals 10 seashells. At the pictorial stage, students are ready to "add the seashells" using pictures rather than shells. Finally, students are able to think abstractly about a concept, using symbols: 7 + 3 = 10 seashells. Fluency with abstract symbols is often the end goal of math instruction, but it should not be the starting place, whether students are adding within 10 or comparing fractions.

As with other instructional strategies, math games range from concrete to pictorial to abstract in approach. In this book, the c-p-a range for each game is listed under The Details in the margin of the right-hand page. When choosing a math game, think about where your students are with respect to a particular concept. If they're just learning a concept or skill, choose a game that has a concrete or pictorial approach. If they understand the concept and are working on fluency, choose a game that relies on abstract representation.

Tips *from the* **Trenches!**

Take the time to play each game yourself with children in your own family, a neighbor's kids, or a small group of students in your class. That way, you'll be familiar with the game and confident using it with an entire classroom of eager mathematicians. Playing the game ahead of class also gives you an opportunity to develop good, thought-provoking questions to ask during play.

Part I: Why, How & When to Use Math Games provides advice on integrating purposeful play into your math instruction. Look for guidance on differentiating games, suggestions for using math games as assessment tools, and ideas for inviting your students' families to join the fun.

All games support Common Core State Standards for Mathematics. The chart on pages 20 to 24 lists which games can be used to address various CCSS clusters and mathematical practices for grades K to 5.

Correlation to CCSS Clusters & Mathematical Practices

COMMON CORE CONTENT CLUSTER	PLAY AS A CLASS	PLAY IN PAIRS OR GROUPS	PLAY ALONE
GRADE K			
K.CC.A Know number names and the count sequence.	Games 2, 3		
K.CC.B Count to tell the number of objects.		Game 17	Game 35
K.CC.C Compare numbers.	Game 3		
K.OA.A Understand addition as putting together and adding to, and understand subtraction as taking apart and taking from.	Game 3	Game 19	
	Games 1, 3, 4	Games 16, 18	Games 32, 33, 36, 38
K.NBT.A Work with numbers 11–19 to gain foundations for place value.	Game 3		
K.G.A Reason with shapes and their attributes.			Game 34
GRADE 1			
1.OA.B Understand and apply properties of operations and the relationship between addition and subtraction.	Game 3		Game 37
1.OA.C Add and subtract within 20.	Games 1, 3, 6	Games 16, 19, 20, 21, 22, 23	Games 32, 33, 36, 38
1.OA.D Work with addition and subtraction equations.	Games 3, 4		Games 36, 38
1.NBT.A Extend the counting sequence.	Games 2, 3		
1.NBT.B Understand place value.	Game 3, 5	Game 17	Game 35
1.NBT.C Use place value understanding and properties of operations to add and subtract.	Game 3		Game 34
1.G.A Reason with shapes and their attributes.		Games 18, 24	
GRADE 2			
2.OA.A Represent and solve problems involving addition and subtraction.			Game 37
2.OA.B Add and subtract within 20.	Games 3, 8,* 9*		
2.OA.C Work with equal groups of objects to gain foundations for multiplication.	Games 1, 3, 6, 8,* 9*	Games 16, 19, 20, 21, 22, 23	Games 32, 33, 36, 38
	Games 3, 8,* 9*		Game 39

20 Math Play • Part I

How the Games Are Organized

Part II: Math Games for Differentiation includes 40 different games arranged by number of student players. Each game has two parts: directions for playing or leading the game on the left-hand page, and tips for using the games in your classroom on the right-hand page.

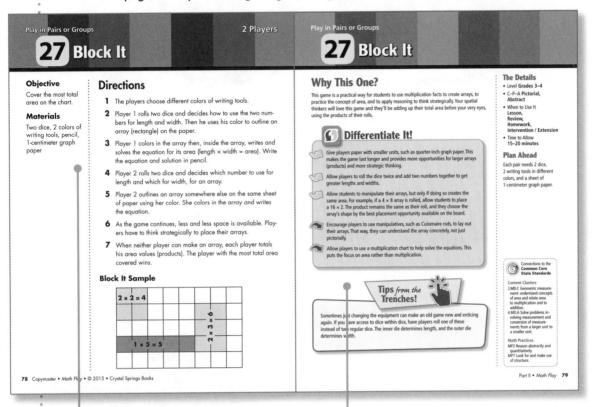

The page on the left has directions for playing the game. Sometimes the directions are addressed to you, the teacher. Other times the directions are given as a copymaster that you may choose to display for the whole class or copy and distribute.

The page on the right has basic information about the game to help you quickly choose and prepare for it, along with ways to differentiate the game by gearing it up to be more challenging or down to be less challenging, depending on your students' grade and readiness levels. Correlations to grade-level CCSS clusters and math practices appear in the margin.

CCSSM Cluster Codes

The original print and pdf editions of *CCSS for Mathematics* use codes for grade level, domain, and standard—for example, "1.G.2" is Grade 1, Geometry, Standard 2. Following the publication of *CCSS for Mathematics*, the CCSS writing team added letter codes to identify the clusters at each grade level in order to facilitate communication and correlation. *Math Play* uses the system that includes cluster codes. In the new system, the same example becomes "1.G.A.2"—Grade 1, Geometry, Cluster A, Standard 2.

On the Left: The Game

Each game has either a set of instructions for leading students in playing the game as a class, or a set of directions that you can copy for student use in class or as homework.

How to Lead the Game instructions are tinted in color so you can easily distinguish them from student Directions, which are in black and white.

The game's number, title, and number of players are listed at the top of the page.

Directions for student use can be copied for use in class or at home.

The game's objective and the materials needed are listed for the players in the margin.

Step-by-step directions for playing the game are provided, including samples of any charts the players may need to make. Games make great home-school connections—send them home for homework the whole family can play!

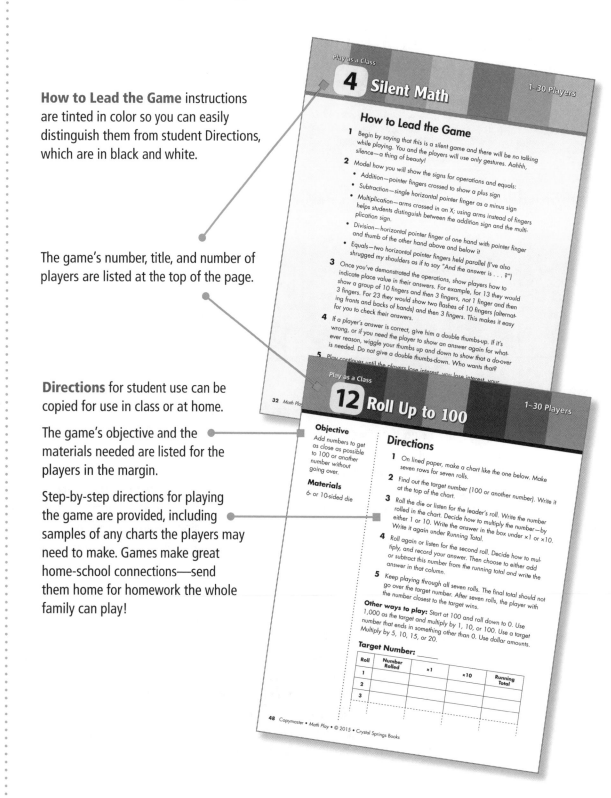

Play as a Class

4 Silent Math

1–30 Players

How to Lead the Game

1 Begin by saying that this is a silent game and there will be no talking while playing. You and the players will use only gestures. Aahhh, silence—a thing of beauty!

2 Model how you will show the signs for operations and equals:
- Addition—pointer fingers crossed to show a plus sign
- Subtraction—single horizontal pointer finger as a minus sign
- Multiplication—arms crossed in an X; using arms instead of fingers helps students distinguish between the addition sign and the multiplication sign.
- Division—horizontal pointer finger of one hand with pointer finger and thumb of the other hand above and below it
- Equals—two horizontal pointer fingers held parallel (I've also shrugged my shoulders as if to say "And the answer is . . . ?")

3 Once you've demonstrated the operations, show players how to indicate place value in their answers. For example, for 13 they would show a group of 10 fingers and then 3 fingers, not 1 finger and then 3 fingers. For 23 they would show two flashes of 10 fingers (alternating fronts and backs of hands) and then 3 fingers. This makes it easy for you to check their answers.

4 If a player's answer is correct, give him a double thumbs-up. If it's wrong, or if you need the player to show an answer again for whatever reason, wiggle your thumbs up and down to show that a do-over is needed. Do not give a double thumbs-down. Who wants that?

5 Play continues until the players lose interest, you lose interest, your

32 Math Pla

Play as a Class

12 Roll Up to 100

1–30 Players

Objective
Add numbers to get as close as possible to 100 or another number without going over.

Materials
6- or 10-sided die

Directions

1 On lined paper, make a chart like the one below. Make seven rows for seven rolls.

2 Find out the target number (100 or another number). Write it at the top of the chart.

3 Roll the die or listen for the leader's roll. Write the number rolled in the chart. Decide how to multiply the number—by either 1 or 10. Write the answer in the box under ×1 or ×10.

4 Roll again or listen for the second roll. Decide how to multiply, and record your answer. Then choose to either add or subtract this number from the running total and write the answer in that column.

5 Keep playing through all seven rolls. The final total should not go over the target number. After seven rolls, the player with the number closest to the target wins.

Other ways to play: Start at 100 and roll down to 0. Use 1,000 as the target and multiply by 1, 10, or 100. Use a target number that ends in something other than 0. Use dollar amounts. Multiply by 5, 10, 15, or 20.

Target Number: _____

Roll	Number Rolled	×1	×10	Running Total
1				
2				
3				

48 Copymaster • Math Play • © 2015 • Crystal Springs Books

On the Right: How to Use the Game

The games in this book are organized by the number of student players. The teacher pages in each section are color-coded so you can tell at a glance which games are best to *Play as a Class* (blue), *Play in Pairs or Groups* (green), or *Play Alone* (purple).

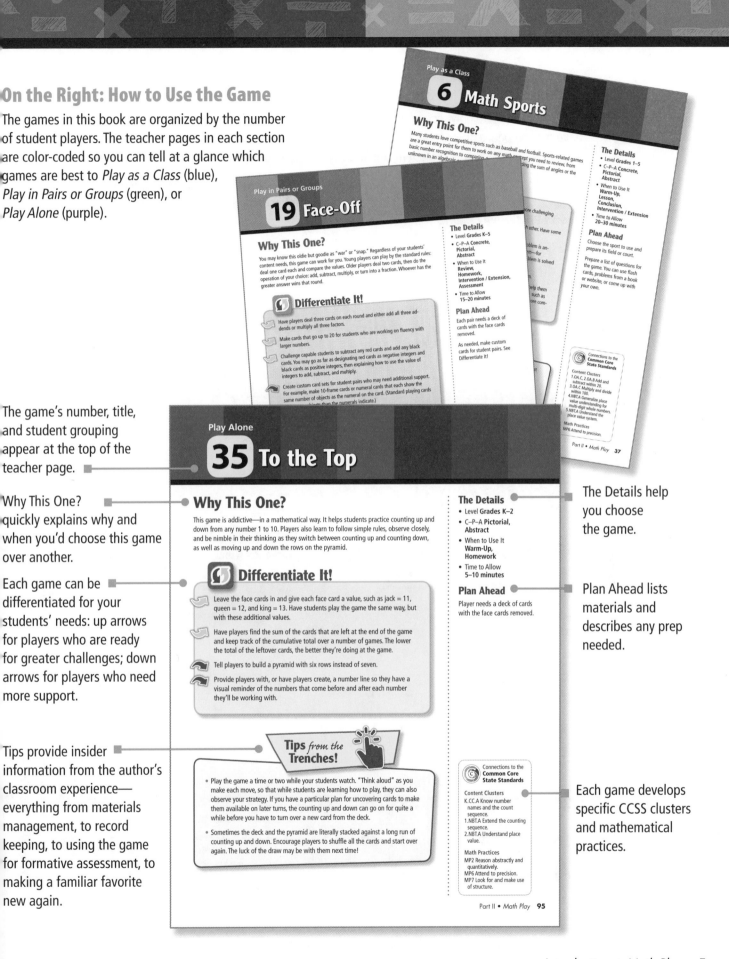

The game's number, title, and student grouping appear at the top of the teacher page.

Why This One? quickly explains why and when you'd choose this game over another.

Each game can be differentiated for your students' needs: up arrows for players who are ready for greater challenges; down arrows for players who need more support.

Tips provide insider information from the author's classroom experience—everything from materials management, to record keeping, to using the game for formative assessment, to making a familiar favorite new again.

The Details help you choose the game.

Plan Ahead lists materials and describes any prep needed.

Each game develops specific CCSS clusters and mathematical practices.

Play as a Class
6 Math Sports

Why This One?

Many students love competitive sports such as baseball and football. Sports-related games are a great entry point for them to work on any math concept you need to review, from basic number recognition to comparing, to finding the sum of angles or the unknown in an algebraic...

The Details
- Level Grades 1–5
- C–P–A **Concrete, Pictorial, Abstract**
- When to Use It **Warm-Up, Lesson, Conclusion, Intervention / Extension**
- Time to Allow **20–30 minutes**

Plan Ahead

Choose the sport to use and prepare its field or court.

Prepare a list of questions for the game. You can use flash cards, problems from a book or website, or come up with your own.

Connections to the Common Core State Standards

Content Clusters
1.OA.C.2,OA.B Add and subtract within 20
3.OA.C Multiply and divide within 100
4.NBT.A Generalize place value understanding for multi-digit whole numbers.
5.NBT.A Understand the place value system.

Math Practices
MP6 Attend to precision.

Part II • Math Play **37**

Play in Pairs or Groups
19 Face-Off

Why This One?

You may know this oldie but goodie as "war" or "snap." Regardless of your students' content needs, this game can work for you. Young players can play by the standard rules: deal one card each and compare the values. Older players deal two cards, then do the operation of your choice: add, subtract, multiply, or turn into a fraction. Whoever has the greater answer wins that round.

Differentiate It!

Have players deal three cards on each round and either add all three addends or multiply all three factors.

Make cards that go up to 20 for students who are working on fluency with larger numbers.

Challenge capable students to subtract any red cards and add any black cards. You may go as far as designating red cards as negative integers and black cards as positive integers, then explaining how to use the value of integers to add, subtract, and multiply.

Create custom card sets for student pairs who may need additional support. For example, make 10-frame cards or numeral cards that each show the same number of objects as the numeral on the card. (Standard playing cards...)

The Details
- Level Grades K–5
- C–P–A **Concrete, Pictorial, Abstract**
- When to Use It **Review, Homework, Intervention / Extension, Assessment**
- Time to Allow **15–20 minutes**

Plan Ahead

Each pair needs a deck of cards with the face cards removed.

As needed, make custom cards for student pairs. See Differentiate It!

Play Alone
35 To the Top

Why This One?

This game is addictive—in a mathematical way. It helps students practice counting up and down from any number 1 to 10. Players also learn to follow simple rules, observe closely, and be nimble in their thinking as they switch between counting up and counting down, as well as moving up and down the rows on the pyramid.

Differentiate It!

Leave the face cards in and give each face card a value, such as jack = 11, queen = 12, and king = 13. Have students play the game the same way, but with these additional values.

Have players find the sum of the cards that are left at the end of the game and keep track of the cumulative total over a number of games. The lower the total of the leftover cards, the better they're doing at the game.

Tell players to build a pyramid with six rows instead of seven.

Provide players with, or have players create, a number line so they have a visual reminder of the numbers that come before and after each number they'll be working with.

Tips from the Trenches!

- Play the game a time or two while your students watch. "Think aloud" as you make each move, so that while students are learning how to play, they can also observe your strategy. If you have a particular plan for uncovering cards to make them available on later turns, the counting up and down can go on for quite a while before you have to turn over a new card from the deck.

- Sometimes the deck and the pyramid are literally stacked against a long run of counting up and down. Encourage players to shuffle all the cards and start over again. The luck of the draw may be with them next time!

The Details
- Level **Grades K–2**
- C–P–A **Pictorial, Abstract**
- When to Use It **Warm-Up, Homework**
- Time to Allow **5–10 minutes**

Plan Ahead

Player needs a deck of cards with the face cards removed.

Connections to the Common Core State Standards

Content Clusters
K.CC.A Know number names and the count sequence.
1.NBT.A Extend the counting sequence.
2.NBT.A Understand place value.

Math Practices
MP2 Reason abstractly and quantitatively.
MP6 Attend to precision.
MP7 Look for and make use of structure.

Part II • Math Play **95**

At the End: Rubrics and Game Boards

Most games require only dice, playing cards, and perhaps paper and pencil. A handful of games have a game board or scorecard, which are provided in **Part III, Copymasters & Resources.** This section also includes a student productivity rubric, a student game reflection sheet, and a student progress tracking sheet.

Math Play Student Productivity Rubric

Oops (1)
- off task
- little or no effort
- didn't help others
- disrespectful
- dependent
- loud!
- didn't use tools
- no evidence

So-So (2)
- off and on task
- did the basics, but with little effort
- kind of helped others
- sometimes respectful
- sometimes independent
- high and low noise levels
- used some tools
- a little evidence

Great! (3)
- mostly on task
- did the basics
- tried to help others
- respectful most of the time
- usually independent; tried to persevere
- good noise level most of the time
- used tools appropriately
- good evidence

Wow!! (4)
- on task the entire time
- looked for a challenge
- helped others a lot
- always respectful
- independent; persevered and problem-solved
- used appropriate noise level
- used tools strategically and appropriately
- good evidence and thought about others' evidence

108 Copymaster •

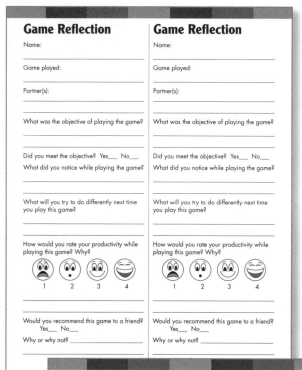

Game Reflection

Name:
_____

Game played:
_____

Partner(s):
_____

What was the objective of playing the game?
_____

Did you meet the objective? Yes___ No___
What did you notice while playing the game?
_____

What will you try to do differently next time you play this game?
_____

How would you rate your productivity while playing this game? Why?

1   2   3   4
_____

Would you recommend this game to a friend?
Yes___ No___
Why or why not? _____

Game Reflection

Name:
_____

Game played:
_____

Partner(s):
_____

What was the objective of playing the game?
_____

Did you meet the objective? Yes___ No___
What did you notice while playing the game?
_____

What will you try to do differently next time you play this game?
_____

How would you rate your productivity while playing this game? Why?

1   2   3   4
_____

Would you recommend this game to a friend?
Yes___ No___
Why or why not? _____

Game 26 Four in a Row Game Board

1. Player 1 covers two factors in the row above the game board with two paper clips, then covers the product of the factors with a playing piece.
2. Player 2 moves one paper clip to a different factor, then covers the product of the factors with a playing piece.
3. Players take turns. The first player to get four products in a row wins.

Factors: 0 1 2 3 4 5 6 7 8 9

1	2	3	4	5	6
7	8	9	10	12	14
15	16	18	20	21	24
25	27	28	30	32	35
36	40	42	45	48	49
54	56	63	64	72	81

114 Copymaster • Math Play • © 2015 • Crystal Springs Books

Game 25 Ninety-Eight Card Values

King
!
Take value straight to 98.

3
←
Reverse direction of play.

4
+0
Worth 0; keep current total the same.

10
–10
Subtract 10 from current total.

Queen or Jack
+10
Add 10 to current total.

Ace
+1 or +11
Add 1 or add 11 (player's choice).

- Number cards not listed in the chart add their face value to the total.
- Cards 3 and 4 do *not* add to the total. They do only what's listed in the chart.
- Remember to draw a card at the end of each turn.

Copymaster • Math Play • © 2015 • Crystal Springs Books 113

PART I

Why, How & When to Use Math Games

Games as an Instructional Strategy

Imagine a classroom that comes alive as students have the chance to experience a math lesson through the lens of a game. Students are mastering math facts, developing conceptual understanding, and applying mathematical practices, even as they are competing, collaborating, and having fun. Meanwhile, the teacher is gathering important data to help drive instruction.

Games are a valid and effective tool to use in everyday mathematical instruction, not just as a reward, time filler, or Friday afternoon treat. They are a purposeful choice made by the teacher to enhance instruction and place learning in the hands of students—sometimes as the lesson, sometimes as an intervention or extension, sometimes as homework, and sometimes as a way to keep all students meaningfully engaged while the teacher works with individuals.

All of this takes planning. For games to fulfill their potential as instructional tools, they must be thoroughly and thoughtfully connected to student outcomes. We can't just pull games from our files because they're fun. We must choose the right game for the right student at the right time. We need to first ask ourselves, "What do I want my students to be better at tomorrow?" and next ask, "Which game will help my students get there?" Then, when the class is playing a game we've chosen, we're ready to answer the question "Why are you playing this game today?" whether it's posed by a student, a parent, or an administrator.

Connecting Games to the Common Core

Ideally, students should know what math they're mastering while playing a game. How can they reach a target if they don't know what it is? Let students know exactly what the Common Core math standards say they should be learning. Make a poster of the CCSS clusters and standards within each domain for your class's grade level, or provide copies for students to keep in their notebooks. Refer to the standards as they learn new math skills and concepts.

Connecting to Clusters: As students learn a new game, challenge them to figure out which content cluster(s) the game addresses and to justify their answers. (You have this information in the CCSS box in the bottom corner of each game's right-hand page.) Acknowledge that some games address more than one cluster or even more than one domain. After students have played a game, have them write the game's name next to the content cluster on their copy of the CCSS standards, or use a sticky note to put it on the class poster. Students will see the connection between the games they're playing and the learning they're doing.

Connecting to Mathematical Practices: Explicitly connecting these games to the eight Mathematical Practices is another way to ensure that students understand what they gain when they play. Some games require perseverance, which is the essence of Mathematical Practice 1. Others make use of repeated reasoning (Practice 8), and still others ask students to use tools appropriately and strategically (Practice 5). As with the clusters, the practices supported by a game are listed in the CCSS box in the bottom corner of the right-hand page.

Right Game, Right Time, Right Reason

When you're considering when to use games from this book, or even games of your own, you need to think about the amount of time it will take to teach and play the game, the materials required, and how long it will take to hand out those materials. You should also consider the complexity of the game, how long it will take to teach if this is the first time playing it, and the level of excitement it will generate. In my class, if we started class with a game like BACON (pages 44 to 45), it would get students all riled up. Bringing them back to focus on something else was a challenge, so I learned to save it for the end of the day, or right before lunch. Choosing the right games for a particular time of day was one of those things I learned over the years by trial and *big* error!

Games for Concrete–Pictorial–Abstract

When students are new to a concept, they need to move and manipulate concrete objects. For example, counting 7 seashells and then counting 3 more seashells shows in a concrete way that 7 plus 3 equals 10 seashells. At the pictorial stage, students are ready to "add the seashells" using pictures rather than shells. Finally, students are able to think abstractly about a concept, using symbols: $7 + 3 = 10$ seashells. Fluency with abstract symbols is often the end goal of math instruction, but it should not be the starting place, whether students are adding within 10 or comparing fractions.

As with other instructional strategies, math games range from concrete to pictorial to abstract in approach. In this book, the c-p-a range for each game is listed under The Details in the margin of the right-hand page. When choosing a math game, think about where your students are with respect to a particular concept. If they're just learning a concept or skill, choose a game that has a concrete or pictorial approach. If they understand the concept and are working on fluency, choose a game that relies on abstract representation.

Tips *from the* **Trenches!**

Take the time to play each game yourself with children in your own family, a neighbor's kids, or a small group of students in your class. That way, you'll be familiar with the game and confident using it with an entire classroom of eager mathematicians. Playing the game ahead of class also gives you an opportunity to develop good, thought-provoking questions to ask during play.

Differentiating Games

The Common Core State Standards give specific grade-level expectations in math for your students. But when have you ever had a class that starts out with every child working at grade level? They're all over the place: some are below grade level, some are at grade level, and some are above. Navigating a classroom where student abilities are so diverse is a central challenge of teaching. Games can help! With math games, one size does not immediately fit all, any more than one-size-fits-all clothing fulfills that promise. But you can differentiate the same game to meet multiple Common Core State Standards across several grade levels and to meet the needs of students working at various levels within the same grade. Game alterations are much simpler than clothing alterations.

Let's look at differentiating the game Face-Off (pages 62 to 63). You may know this card game as "war" or "snap"; I've renamed it in honor of a classroom full of hockey fans. In the

Differentiating Face-Off: One Game, Many Learning Goals

GRADE LEVEL	COMMON CORE CLUSTER	CARD DECK MODIFICATION	VARIATIONS
Kindergarten	K.CC.C Compare numbers.	Provide teacher-made decks with numerals and pictorial representations, such as a particular number of items, 5-frame cards, 10-frame cards, or dots arranged in both regular and irregular subitizing patterns.	K.CC.C Each player turns over one teacher-made card and compares to find out which is larger. Provide manipulatives or a number line for scaffolded support.
Grade 1	1.OA.C Add and subtract within 20. 1.OA.D Work with addition and subtraction equations. 1.NBT.B Understand place value.	Remove the face cards from a traditional deck and have aces equal 1, or use a deck with multiple cards showing the numerals 1 to 9 and corresponding numbers of dots or items.	1.OA.C Each player turns over two cards and finds the sum of the cards. The larger sum wins. Or each player turns over two cards and finds the difference (omitting negative numbers). The larger difference wins. 1.OA.D Have players say or write the equations as they play the 1.OA.C variation. 1.NBT.B Each player turns over two cards and arranges them to make the greatest possible two-digit number to win. For more advanced players, use three cards and go to the hundreds place.
Grade 2	2.OA.B Add and subtract within 20. 2.NBT.A Understand place value. 2.MD.C Work with time and money.	Remove the face cards from a traditional deck. Use decks of flash cards (or create cards) that present concepts related to time and money. Include both pictorial and abstract representations.	2.OA.B, 2.NBT.A See the variations for 1.OA.C and 1.NBT.B above. 2.MD.C Using time and money flash cards or teacher-made cards, each player turns over one card. The player with the higher value of money or the earlier time wins the round.

traditional version of the game, two players are each dealt half a deck of cards. Each player then turns over one card. The player with the greater number takes both cards. A face-off occurs when both players turn over cards of equal value. Each then lays down two more cards and turns the next card faceup. The player with the greater faceup card value takes the entire pile of eight cards. Play continues until one player is out of cards.

Put on two new lenses to view this game: Common Core and Differentiation. The chart below gives examples of how this one game can be adjusted to support math clusters from kindergarten to grade 5. (In fact, I think it can go all the way to grade 8 or even higher.) You'll need some deck modifications, but the same rules apply. And the variations don't just help you to adjust the game across grade levels; they also help you to differentiate, so the same game can be used to assist players in achieving different goals at the same time and in the same classroom.

GRADE LEVEL	COMMON CORE CLUSTER	CARD DECK MODIFICATION	VARIATIONS
Grade 3	3.OA.C Multiply and divide within 100. 3.NF.A Develop understanding of fractions as numbers. 3.MD.C Geometric measurement: understand concepts of area and relate area to multiplication and to addition.	Assign values to the face cards, such as jack = 10, queen = 11, and king = 12. Create card decks that represent fractions both as pictures and as numerals. Make card decks with a mix of pictorial and abstract representations: some cards have rectangular arrays showing area, while others have numerical values for length and width without any pictures.	3.OA.C Using a regular deck of cards, each player turns over two cards and finds the product of the numbers. Largest product wins. 3.NF.A Each player turns over one fraction card. Whichever fraction is closer to 1 wins. If the two fractions are equivalent, a face-off ensues. 3.MD.C Each player turns over one area card. The player with the larger area wins. For a real challenge, give areas in different units—for example, players compare 16 feet versus 64 inches.
Grade 4	4.OA.B Gain familiarity with factors and multiples. 4.NF.C Understand decimal notation for fractions, and compare decimal fractions. 4.MD.C Geometric measurement: understand concepts of angle and measure angles.	Assign values to the face cards, such as jack = 10, queen = 11, and king = 12. Create two card decks, one with the numbers 1 to 10 and the other with only 10s. Create cards with various angle measurements.	4.OA.B See the variation for 3.OA.C above. 4.NF.C Each player takes a card from the 1 to 10 deck and a card from the 10s deck, uses it to make a fractional representation "out of 10," then records the fraction as a decimal. The player with the value closer to 1 wins. 4.MD.C Using a deck with angles and their measurements, each player turns over a card, names the angle (acute, straight, obtuse, right), and then measures it using a protractor. The player with the larger angle measurement wins the round and keeps all the cards.
Grade 5	5.NBT.A Understand the place value system.	Remove the face cards from a traditional deck. Provide a decimal point on a sticky note with each card deck.	5.NBT.A Players put the decimal point on the table. Each player draws one, two, or three cards and, using the decimal point, arranges them to make a number. The player whose number is closer to 1 wins.

Games as Assessment Tools

I've always believed that if you expect it, you should assess it. So if you expect to use your time to teach a math game and the students' time to play it, you need to assess their progress as a result of playing it. The key with assessment and games is to use the time while students are actively engaged in a task to gather data you will need to lead them to the next steps in their learning. How can you do this?

Look, Listen & Ask

Games in progress are a prime opportunity to eavesdrop intentionally for formative assessment purposes. You can observe students in any game grouping, from whole class to individual. For example, in the card game You Never Lose (pages 88 to 89), players find number bonds of 10. While a student is playing this game, observe which bonds of 10 he notices right away, which he consistently misses, and which he struggles with but eventually gets. These observations are data you can use to make decisions regarding additional instruction.

Asking questions while observing is a good way to get at the heart of a student's understanding—with the added bonus of modeling how to ask thoughtful questions. Well-chosen, open-ended questions also help address the Mathematical Practices, especially the ones related to reasoning and critiquing thought processes. Some of my favorite open-ended math questions include the following:

- Why are you correct? Can you show me?
- Can you think of another way to solve it?
- How did you know to try that?
- What would you do next time?

Start with questions like these and come up with some of your own, too.

Hold Kids Accountable

Another level of accountability is to ask students to reflect on the games they're playing. I suggest using a self-reflection list that holds students accountable for their behavior as well as their math. But I like to call it "productivity" rather than "behavior," because if students choose inappropriate behavior, their game play will not be productive. Including behavior in self-reflection is a good way to remind students that their personal work ethic is an important component of their math learning.

I've provided a reflection sheet that you can use on page 109. I don't recommend having students fill out a reflection sheet every time they play a game, but I do think it's a good idea to do so periodically as a purposeful way to check on their progress. For the earliest learners, reflection sheets are less practical. A quick verbal check-in is one way to collect data. Ask a question related to a student's math learning starting with "Can you . . ." or "Did you . . . ," and follow up with one about behavior starting with "How well did you . . ." Kids can respond with a thumbs-up or thumbs-down.

Track Students' Progress

When games become a regular part of your classroom experience, you'll want to keep a written record of students' math progress through games, just as you would track their progress through tasks, quizzes, or any other classroom activity. A simple chart like the one below works fine. Or maybe you'd rather write your observations directly on the students' record sheets or scorecards before handing them back. Whatever works for you is what works best.

Be specific with your feedback. Instead of "good job," write comments such as "You're really quick at making bonds of 10" or "Good use of 10-frames to make bonds of 10." The specificity will help both you and your students as you assess their proficiency levels.

Student Name	Common Core Goal	Observations	Next Step(s)
Jason			
Liu			
Eduardo			

You might want to use a separate tracking sheet for each student instead of or in addition to the class list shown above. One example is the Student Progress Tracking Sheet on page 110. With this kind of record, you can see each individual's progress, make notes to yourself about next steps, and pull that data out at parent-teacher conferences or when compiling a summative assessment at the end of a marking period.

Student Progress Tracking Sheet

Student Name _____

Assessment Data _____

	STRENGTHS			GOALS	
Date	Intervention, Instruction, or Extension	Observation	Proficiency Level (1, 2, 3, 4)		Next Steps

Managing Materials & Students

Some teachers avoid playing games in their classrooms because of the logistical nightmare of materials and student management. Often, nightmares are worse than daytime reality. Don't let your bad dreams get in your way.

Simplify Game Materials

My criteria for games are simplicity and minimal manipulatives. Over the years, I've tried several organizational strategies and have narrowed managing manipulatives down to a few main principles.

Keep It Together: Keep all the manipulatives of the same type in the same tub. I have a tub of regular dice, a tub of decks of cards, a tub of place-value dice, and so forth. Keep the tubs at student level, clearly labeled, and accessible at all times. This helps kids choose an appropriate tool and use it strategically, which the Mathematical Practices ask them to do.

Emphasize Tools Not Toys: Before any manipulatives are used, students need to understand the difference between manipulatives as "toys" and manipulatives as "math tools." Discuss and model in advance what it looks like when dice are being used as toys (for stacking, building, making pictures) and when they are being used as number-generating tools (rolling them for games such as Roll High, Roll Low or Greedy). For younger learners, it can be useful to have a poster or image with pictures illustrating the difference: "Right now, these dice are toys" and "Now these dice are tools."

Assemble in Advance: Assemble "tool kits" of all the materials students need to play each game and store them in a resealable plastic bag or pencil box. This might mean pulling some materials out of the tubs, but you may find that this approach works better for you. Keep the

Tips *from the* Trenches!

- I used to spend hours cutting out cute things, laminating them, and cutting them out again. Then I had to make sure none of those adorable game pieces got lost! Those days are over for me. Now I choose games with simple materials that are easy to manage and replace, such as cards and dice. That way, I can focus on student learning, not the cuteness factor.

- Try color-coding material kits for differentiation. Choose a specific color of dice for a certain skill grouping, or use sticky dots on toolboxes so you can say to students, "You'll be playing from the blue boxes" or "You'll use the green dice today."

tool kits where they're easily accessible to students, so kids can "grab and go" when they have the chance. Periodically, do a big clean-and-sort as a class: check all the kits for missing items, make sure the decks have all their cards, and problem-solve if there are missing materials.

Simplify Game Directions

The simplest way to teach a game is to model it for students first, then let them play it. This is helpful whether the game is played as a whole class, in pairs or groups, or individually. Once they've played a game, students often need only a quick reminder to remember the rules and start again. (We adults tend to have a hard time remembering all the rules to a game. Try asking your students if you're unsure of the details!) The kind of reminder you provide depends on the reading level of your students.

Directions for Nonreaders: A simple way to remind young players of a game's structure is to make signs similar to the ones shown in the illustration. These signs include the game's name, the materials kids need to play, and how many people can play. Post these signs in a prominent place and refer to them often. When you're differentiating, signs can be a way to keep track of who gets to play what. Place a sticky note with students' names next to the games they should play during a particular week. Change it up as students' skills develop.

Simple signs remind players what the game is, what materials they need to play it, why they're playing it, and whom they can play it with.

Directions for Readers: For students who read independently, provide printed directions as a reference, either before or after you model and play the game. When I ran my own classroom, I put students in charge of managing game directions. At the start of the year, we had a set of three-pronged folders to make class game books; no one folder belonged to any one student, and I had a few more folders than students in the class, just in case. As I taught a game, I handed out three-hole-punched copies of the directions for students to add to the folders. Throughout the year, students could grab a game folder to refer to the rules of a particular game, find the materials, or follow a template to make the game's scorecard. At the end of the year, all the students took home a folder with all the game directions so they could play over the summer. I think some of those game folders are still in the kids' bedrooms, family campers, and game cupboards!

Simplify Student Groupings

The games in this book are organized according to suggested group size. But for games to be effective, group size and makeup must support learning in *your* classroom, with *your* students. You may find that for your class, some games work better with a different number of players. You may discover that this year's students follow along better when they play as a class, whereas last year's worked better in small groups. You may find that certain students simply don't focus on math when they're in the same group. Knowledge is power, so be a purposeful eavesdropper as you get to know your students and their work habits.

Whatever size group you choose, you need a way to get players into groups. Here are a few favorite strategies that work for me.

Quick & Easy: One of my favorite strategies for partners and small groups is using "shoulder buddies." This is very easy. I love easy! Each student partners with the person whose shoulder is nearest to hers—rather than the person she may *want* to play with, who's across the room. This grouping is very low prep and does not involve much moving around. When you need small groups, have two nearby pairs of shoulder buddies make one "family."

Preplanned: Sometimes it's important to have more control over student groupings. Here's one way. If you're handing out preprinted scorecards for a game, mark them with colored sticky dots and ask players to find other kids with the same color. Hand out papers with certain colors to specific students, or write their names on the colored dots and put them right on the papers. That way, *you're* in control—whether you're grouping by ability, by gender, or to mitigate undesirable behavior.

Season & Clock Partners: The basic idea here is that students choose multiple buddies to partner with on a regular basis. For season partners, kids select a buddy for each season of the year—the catch being that both partners must name each other for a particular season. For example, if Isabelle writes Olivia's name for fall, then Olivia must write Isabelle's name for fall, too. When you say, "Find your fall partner for today's game," Isabelle and Olivia pair up. (And yes, you can use fall pairings in the spring! The seasons are just a way for students to find their partners.)

Clock partners are similar to season partners, but this grouping scheme offers the chance for more choices. Provide a printed clock face. Each student writes a classmate's name next

Tips *from the* Trenches!

If you use a strategy such as clock or season partners over and over, have students tape or glue their partner information in their math notebooks for reference. But first record all the pairings for yourself. That way, if a student conveniently misplaces his chart of preferred math partners, you can fill him in.

Tips *from the* Trenches!

No matter what the grouping, model and explain what a game should look and sound like—then expect that behavior from all players. Before my students played a game, I'd hang up a T chart with a big eye on one side and a big ear on the other, then invite the students to contribute ideas about what we should *see* and what we should *hear* while working together. It's better to focus on *shoulds* rather than *should nots*.

to each number on the clock. For younger students, use 3, 6, 9, and 12 o'clock. If you're working with intermediate students, you can use every hour on the clock. Make sure students understand that they may be asked to play with their 5 o'clock partner at 10 o'clock!

It's in the Cards: Try using playing cards as a quick grouping technique. Hand out cards randomly and have students form groups based on your criteria. For example, have all the fives form a group, or have players join with others who hold the same suit. You could have students make groups based on who is holding even or odd numbers, or join with other students to make a four-card run.

With forethought, you can create long-term groupings that associate players' personal traits with specific suits and cards. For example, Aces are students who struggle with fact fluency, and Clubs are boys, so an Ace of Clubs is a boy who struggles with fact fluency. Hand out the appropriate cards for students to tape inside their notebooks or on their desks. Then, when you need groups for a specific game, you'll have groups with similar needs without really thinking too hard.

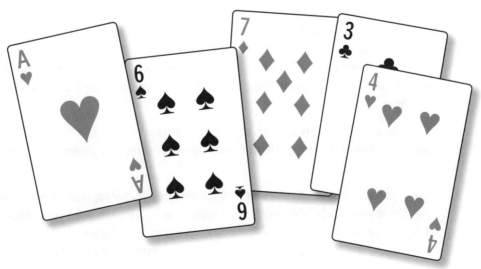

Connecting Home & School

Teachers and parents alike want students to be engaged mathematicians. Both parties want students to be successful, proficient, and working at grade level. And everyone—adults and children—wants to avoid nightly battles over math homework. So how can you accomplish all this?

Assigning games as math homework is a win-win option. Games give parents an opportunity to *support* instruction without having to relearn math so they can *provide* instruction. You get students to practice skills at home, and parents don't have to beg, plead, and argue with their kids to get them to do their homework.

But don't leave this home-school connection to chance. Make it happen. It's worth creating a strong home-classroom community, and games are a fantastically powerful way to do this.

The first step is to teach parents how to play the games. Learning how to play these games helps parents understand what's expected from these nontraditional homework assignments. It also helps you head off any complaints along the lines of "If it's a game, it isn't serious." Any adult who has to refresh old math skills to play a math game with a child will find out that games are real practice!

There are several ways to engage parents, depending on your local community.

Host Family Game Events

Feed them, and they will come! The school provides the food and the game materials, and the parents provide the kids.

One format that works well is "Dice and Dinner." One teacher sits at each grade-level table, ready to teach math games that use dice. The parents and children eat pizza, roam around the game tables, and learn how to play the games together. Or if the children have played a game in class, they can be the experts and teach their parents. When the families are finished, they leave through a designated door, where they receive a bag of dice and directions to all the games they just played. I've been involved in these events. The turnout is fantastic, the feedback is incredibly positive, and most important, it sets the stage for a more engaged environment for math, both at school and at home.

A similar event is "Cards and Cookies." Same concept as Dice and Dinner, but cards are given out to families at the end of an evening of eating cookies and playing math games that use playing cards.

The importance of timing in these events cannot be overstated. Hosting one evening early in the school year builds relationships and momentum that will benefit your students throughout the year. Another event near the end of the school year encourages reflection on what's been learned and sets the stage for continued practice during summer vacation.

Plan, plan, plan in advance for a successful event. Get your administration and colleagues on board early in the process. Reserve space in the school. Check local requirements for serving food. Arrange for on-site babysitting for younger children so that older siblings can have their parents' full attention. Invite local businesses to donate food or the cost of the game materials families take home, and remember to give the businesses credit for doing so.

Post Games Online

No time for an event? You can still teach parents how to play the games. One teacher I know utilizes her students' dual love of technology and math games. She makes videos that model how to play each game, then posts them online, where parents and students can see them. There is no need to show students' faces. Just set up a camera to capture their hands as they play the game while you record the voice-over directions yourself. Post the videos and written directions on your class's website or blog, if you have one. Or if the file is small enough, attach it to an email sent directly to parents. You will need to get parental permission for your student models even if only their hands are showing.

Involve & Inform

In the classroom, parents are great helpers for managing your differentiated environment. Parent volunteers aren't responsible for teaching; they just play games with the students and help with recording and crowd management. Their assistance frees you up to do data collection while your students are playing. You can also use parent-supported game time as a meaningful distraction while you pull out a small group to reteach or extend a concept.

Set parents up for success. Communication is the key. Keep your parent community in the loop as you work with familiar math games and introduce new ones. Send parent letters or emails with news about a game to discuss with children, or with instructions for a new game to try at home. Post information on social media sites that parents can access, such as your class blog or your school's Facebook page or website.

As you embark on game playing to engage your diverse learners, remember three things: keep it simple, keep it focused on learning, and set everyone up for success in math.

Oh, have fun, too!

Correlation to CCSS Clusters & Mathematical Practices

COMMON CORE CONTENT CLUSTER	PLAY AS A CLASS	PLAY IN PAIRS OR GROUPS	PLAY ALONE
GRADE K			
K.CC.A Know number names and the count sequence.	Games 2, 3	Game 17	Game 35
K.CC.B Count to tell the number of objects.	Game 3		
K.CC.C Compare numbers.	Game 3	Game 19	
K.OA.A Understand addition as putting together and adding to, and understand subtraction as taking apart and taking from.	Games 1, 3, 4	Games 16, 18	Games 32, 33, 36, 38
K.NBT.A Work with numbers 11–19 to gain foundations for place value.	Game 3		Game 34
K.G.A Reason with shapes and their attributes.			Game 37
GRADE 1			
1.OA.B Understand and apply properties of operations and the relationship between addition and subtraction.	Game 3		
1.OA.C Add and subtract within 20.	Games 1, 3, 6	Games 16, 19, 20, 21, 22, 23	Games 32, 33, 36, 38
1.OA.D Work with addition and subtraction equations.	Games 3, 4		Games 36, 38
1.NBT.A Extend the counting sequence.	Games 2, 3	Game 17	Game 35
1.NBT.B Understand place value.	Game 3, 5		Game 34
1.NBT.C Use place value understanding and properties of operations to add and subtract.	Game 3	Games 18, 24	
1.G.A Reason with shapes and their attributes.			Game 37
GRADE 2			
2.OA.A Represent and solve problems involving addition and subtraction.	Games 3, 8,* 9*		
2.OA.B Add and subtract within 20.	Games 1, 3, 6, 8,* 9*	Games 16, 19, 20, 21, 22, 23	Games 32, 33, 36, 38
2.OA.C Work with equal groups of objects to gain foundations for multiplication.	Games 3, 8,* 9*		Game 39

COMMON CORE CONTENT CLUSTER	PLAY AS A CLASS	PLAY IN PAIRS OR GROUPS	PLAY ALONE
2.NBT.A Understand place value.	Games 2, 3, 5, 7, 8,* 9*	Games 17	Games 34, 35
2.NBT.B Use place value understanding and properties of operations to add and subtract.	Games 3, 4, 8,* 9*	Games 18, 24, 25	Game 40
2.MD.A Measure and estimate lengths in standard units.	Games 8,* 9*		
2.MD.B Relate addition and subtraction to length.	Games 8,* 9*		
2.MD.C Work with time and money.	Games 8,* 9*		
2.MD.D Represent and interpret data.	Games 8,* 9*		
2.G.A Reason with shapes and their attributes.	Games 8,* 9*		Game 37
GRADE 3			
3.OA.A Represent and solve problems involving multiplication and division.	Games 3, 8,* 9,* 13,** 14**	Game 30	Game 39
3.OA.B Understand properties of multiplication and the relationship between multiplication and division.	Games 3, 8,* 9,* 13,** 14**	Game 30	Game 40
3.OA.C Multiply and divide within 100.	Games 1, 3, 4, 6, 8,* 9,* 13,** 14**	Game 19, 23, 26, 30	Games 36, 38
3.OA.D Solve problems involving the four operations, and identify and explain patterns in arithmetic.	Games 3, 8,* 9,* 13,** 14**	Game 30	
3.NBT.A Use place value understanding and properties of operations to perform multi-digit arithmetic.	Games 3, 5, 8,* 9,* 10, 11, 12, 13,** 14**	Games 17, 18, 24, 25, 29, 30, 31	
3.NF.A Develop understanding of fractions as numbers.	Games 8,* 9,* 13,** 14**		
3.MD.A Solve problems involving measurement and estimation of intervals of time, liquid volumes, and masses of objects.	Games 8,* 9,* 13,** 14**		
3.MD.B Represent and interpret data.	Games 8,* 9,* 13,** 14**		

* Games 8 and 9 are vocabulary games that can be used for any cluster grades 2 to 5.

** Games 13 and 14 have students apply mathematical practices and questioning strategies while solving problems and can be used for any cluster grades 3 to 5.

COMMON CORE CONTENT CLUSTER	PLAY AS A CLASS	PLAY IN PAIRS OR GROUPS	PLAY ALONE
3.MD.C Geometric measurement: understand concepts of area and relate area to multiplication and to addition.	Games 8,* 9,* 13,** 14**	Game 27	
3.MD.D Geometric measurement: recognize perimeter as an attribute of plane figures and distinguish between linear and area measures.	Games 8,* 9,* 13,** 14**		
3.G.A Reason with shapes and their attributes.	Games 8,* 9,* 13,** 14**		Game 37
GRADE 4			
4.OA.A Use the four operations with whole numbers to solve problems.	Games 3, 8,* 9,* 13,** 14**	Game 30	Games 39, 40
4.OA.B Gain familiarity with factors and multiples.	Games 2, 3, 8,* 9,* 13,** 14**	Game 30	
4.OA.C Generate and analyze patterns.	Games 3, 8,* 9,* 13,** 14**	Game 30	
4.NBT.A Generalize place value understanding for multi-digit whole numbers.	Games 3, 5, 6, 7, 8,* 9,* 11, 12, 13,** 14**	Games 29, 30	
4.NBT.B Use place value understanding and properties of operations to perform multi-digit arithmetic.	Games 3, 5, 8,* 9,* 10, 13,** 14,** 15	Games 25, 30, 31	Games 36, 38
4.NF.A Extend understanding of fraction equivalence and ordering.	Games 8,* 9,* 13,** 14**	Game 19	
4.NF.B Build fractions from unit fractions by applying and extending previous understandings of operations on whole numbers.	Games 4, 8,* 9,* 13,** 14**		
4.NF.C Understand decimal notation for fractions, and compare decimal fractions.	Games 8,* 9,* 13,** 14**		
4.MD.A Solve problems involving measurement and conversion of measurements from a larger unit to a smaller unit.	Games 8,* 9,* 13,** 14**	Game 27	
4.MD.B Represent and interpret data.	Games 8,* 9,* 13,** 14**		
4.MD.C Geometric measurement: understand concepts of angle and measure angles.	Games 8,* 9,* 13,** 14**	Game 28	

COMMON CORE CONTENT CLUSTER	PLAY AS A CLASS	PLAY IN PAIRS OR GROUPS	PLAY ALONE
4.G.A Draw and identify lines and angles, and classify shapes by properties of their lines and angles.	Games 8,* 9,* 13,** 14**	Game 28	Game 37
GRADE 5			
5.OA.A Write and interpret numerical expressions.	Games 8,* 9,* 13,** 14**	Game 30	Games 36, 38, 40
5.OA.B Analyze patterns and relationships.	Games 8,* 9,* 13,** 14**	Game 30	
5.NBT.A Understand the place value system.	Games 5, 6, 8,* 9,* 13,** 14**	Games 29, 30	
5.NBT.B Perform operations with multi-digit whole numbers and with decimals to hundredths.	Games 5, 8,* 9,* 12, 13,** 14,** 15	Games 30, 31	
5.NF.A Use equivalent fractions as a strategy to add and subtract fractions.	Games 8,* 9,* 13,** 14**	Game 19	
5.NF.B Apply and extend previous understandings of multiplication and division to multiply and divide fractions.	Games 4, 8,* 9,* 13,** 14**		
5.MD.A Convert like measurement units within a given measurement system.	Games 8,* 9,* 13,** 14**		
5.MD.B Represent and interpret data.	Games 8,* 9,* 13,** 14**		
5.MD.C Geometric measurement: understand concepts of volume and relate volume to multiplication and to addition.	Games 8,* 9,* 13,** 14**		
5.G.A Graph points on the coordinate plane to solve real-world and mathematical problems.	Games 8,* 9,* 13,** 14**		
5.G.B Classify two-dimensional figures into categories based on their properties.	Games 8,* 9,* 13,** 14**		Game 37

* Games 8 and 9 are vocabulary games that can be used for any cluster grades 2 to 5.

** Games 13 and 14 have students apply mathematical practices and questioning strategies while solving problems and can be used for any cluster grades 3 to 5.

MATHEMATICAL PRACTICES	PLAY AS A CLASS	PLAY IN PAIRS OR GROUPS	PLAY ALONE
MP1 Make sense of problems and persevere in solving them.	Games 13, 15	Game 30	Game 40
MP2 Reason abstractly and quantitatively.	Games 3, 4, 5, 10, 11, 13	Games 16, 17, 18, 19, 20, 22, 23, 24, 25, 26, 27, 29, 31	Games 34, 35, 37, 39, 40
MP3 Construct viable arguments and critique the reasoning of others.	Games 7, 13, 14, 15	Games 24, 31	
MP4 Model with mathematics.	Game 13	Game 28	Games 34, 39, 40
MP5 Use appropriate tools strategically.	Games 8, 13	Game 28	Game 38
MP6 Attend to precision.	Games 1, 3, 4, 5, 6, 9, 10, 11, 12, 13, 15	Games 16, 18, 19, 20, 21, 22, 23, 24, 25, 26, 28, 29, 30, 31	Games 32, 33, 34, 35, 36, 38, 40
MP7 Look for and make use of structure.	Games 2, 7, 13	Games 20, 25, 27	Games 33, 35, 37
MP8 Look for and express regularity in repeated reasoning.	Games 10, 12, 13	Games 17, 18, 29	Games 32, 33, 38, 39

PART II

Math Games for Differentiation

1 Rock, Paper, Scissors, Math

How to Lead the Game

1 Model the traditional game of rock, paper, scissors.

2 Explain that the class will be playing a math version of this game. Depending on the math fluency goals, players find either a sum or a product of two numbers. Review what a sum or product is.

3 Explain that players move around the room to find a partner. To play, the two partners say together, "Rock, paper, scissors, math," while tapping their fists into their palms—one tap each for rock, paper, scissors. When they say "math," they each "throw" a number of fingers flat on the palm of the other hand.

4 Once they've thrown a number of fingers, players find the sum or product of the two numbers shown on their hands. The first player to say the correct sum or product wins that round. This is where it gets a little loud, but controlled chaos is fun, right?

5 Play continues with the same partner until a player wins two out of three rounds. You know, the old "best out of three."

6 After three rounds, players move on to a new partner—preferably choosing someone who is nearest to them, not dearest to them. Play continues for as long as you allow.

1 Rock, Paper, Scissors, Math

Why This One?

or the wiggle worms (kinesthetic learners) in your room, this game provides both math act fluency practice and movement. Players enjoy the time-tested game of rock, paper, cissors, but instead of "throwing" one of those three items, they use fingers to represent a number. Then, depending on what needs practice, they find either the sum or the product of the two numbers. Focus on sums for addition practice in grades K, 1, and 2 and products for multiplication practice in grade 3.

 ## Differentiate It!

Have players double their "throws" before they find the sum or product.

Tell players to use both hands and throw numbers flat on a table rather than on the other palm. This gives larger addends and larger factors, thus creating larger sums and larger products.

Instruct players to name the numbers and compare their values, rather than adding or multiplying. This approach is especially useful for younger players.

The very youngest players may simply recognize numbers, without comparing or manipulating them. Have each player say the number of fingers his partner throws. The first player to correctly say her partner's number wins that round.

Tips *from the* Trenches!

- Players may end up gravitating toward friends. Make sure all partners focus on getting the math done, not hanging with their recess buddies.

- This game is a great opportunity to explain properties associated with 0 and 1. It can be a hoot letting players discover on their own why they shouldn't throw a 0 (closed fist) when adding or multiplying, or a 1 when multiplying. Once they've figured it out, ask them not to do it anymore.

The Details

- Level **Grades K–3**
- C–P–A **Concrete, Abstract**
- When to Use It **Warm-Up, Conclusion**
- Time to Allow **10–15 minutes**

Plan Ahead

No preparation needed.

Connections to the **Common Core State Standards**

Content Clusters
K.OA.A Understand addition as putting together and adding to, and understand subtraction as taking apart and taking from.
1.OA.C, 2.OA.B Add and subtract within 20.
3.OA.C Multiply and divide within 100.

Math Practices
MP6 Attend to precision.

2 Loud-Soft Count

How to Lead the Game

1 Explain this version of the game "you're getting hotter." One player leaves the room, and an object is hidden. When the player returns, all the other players count by whatever sequence you choose. The counting gets louder as the player gets closer to the hidden object and quieter as the player moves away.

2 Choose an item to hide, a player to find it, and a sequence for the class to count by. The sequence you choose depends on the grade level and learning targets of the class, but some examples are counting by 1s, 2s, 5s, or multiples of any number. Remember to sometimes start from a nonobvious place; for example, count by 10s starting at 16, or count by 2s starting at 7.

3 Have the player who will look for the object leave the room while the class hides the object.

4 When the player reenters the room, the counting starts out quietly. As the player moves closer to the object, the counting gets louder; as the player moves away, it gets softer.

5 When the object has been found, choose a new player and start a new round.

2 Loud-Soft Count

Why This One?

Counting in the early grades and multiples in the intermediate grades are essential skills in using and recognizing the patterns in numbers. But how do you practice these skills in a meaningful way? This modification of the game "you're getting hotter" lets your students have fun while developing fluency with counting, skip counting, and multiples.

 ## Differentiate It!

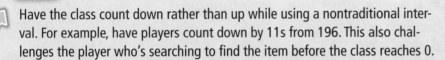

Have the class count down rather than up while using a nontraditional interval. For example, have players count down by 11s from 196. This also challenges the player who's searching to find the item before the class reaches 0.

Have the class count up by fractional amounts, such as counting by fourths or counting by thirds, rather than counting by whole numbers.

Reinforce place-value concepts for larger numbers by counting in increments of 100s or 1000s. This works in both directions; try starting at 100,000 and count down.

Provide visual support for the counting, such as a hundred chart or a number line.

Use this game as an opportunity to practice multiples of specific factors, especially factors that students often struggle with, such as 6, 7, and 8.

 ## Tips *from the* Trenches!

- While players are counting, "conduct" the chant by raising your hand up to indicate getting louder and bringing your hand down to indicate getting softer.

- Make sure the item is "hidden in plain sight" so that as the player gets closer and the counting gets louder, the player is actually able to find it.

The Details

- Level **Grades K–2, 4**

- C–P–A **Abstract**

- When to Use It **Warm-Up, Conclusion**

- Time to Allow **5–10 minutes**

Plan Ahead

Choose an object to hide.

Connections to the **Common Core State Standards**

Content Clusters
K.CC.A Know number names and the count sequence.
1.NBT.A Extend the counting sequence.
2.NBT.A Understand place value.
4.OA.B Gain familiarity with factors and multiples.

Math Practices
MP7 Look for and make use of structure.

3 Math Digits

How to Lead the Game

1 Have players lay 0 to 9 digit cards in order near the top edge of their desks.

2 Read aloud the series of mental math tasks. As you read each task, each player pulls down the digit(s) that make the answer. Here's an example:

Teacher: Start with the number of sides on a triangle.
   Player pulls down a 3.
Teacher: Double that number.
   Player replaces the 3 with a 6.
Teacher: Increase that number by 10.
   Player pulls down a 1, placing it in the tens place to make 16.
Teacher: Divide that number by 4.
   Player replaces both the 1 and the 6 with a 4.
Teacher: Multiply that number by 5.
   Player replaces the 4 with a 2 and a 0 to create 20.
Teacher: Show me your answer.
   Player holds up the 2 and the 0 to show 20.

Pointers

• If an answer uses the same digit twice, such as 22, tell players to shift the digit back and forth to show that it goes in both the ones place and the tens place.

• Keep track of the answer as you give each instruction.

• Roam the room for a formative assessment opportunity. After a certain number of instructions, ask all the players to show their answers. Check for how many are correct.

• This game has no winner, but players feel good knowing they kept up with the correct answer.

3 Math Digits

Why This One?

This game is low prep and can be used for a cumulative review of multiple concepts during the same game. Practice will, indeed, make permanent! You give clues that prompt players to mentally manipulate numbers based on your commands. Isn't that fun? Their math is your command! You can check answers from time to time for an informal assessment. Plus, this is a quiet response game. Aahhh!

Differentiate It!

Create a set of prompts that challenge capable students.

Initially, the digit cards are a nice scaffold. But as students learn the game, challenge them to follow the prompts mentally.

Deliver prompts with less wait time.

To practice counting, show a number of objects and have players pull down the matching digit card.

Allow more wait time between prompts.

Do a series of prompts one-on-one so you can track each student's progress at each step.

Tips *from the* Trenches!

- Discourage grunting when players lose track and cheering when they get the right answer. Say each task once and only once to encourage active listening. Encourage players to close their eyes to facilitate visualization.

- Encourage students to be practical problem-solvers. For example, a player can re-create a lost digit card from a piece of scrap paper.

- Have students write their own prompts for use the next day. List the vocabulary and concepts to include, differentiating for individual students as appropriate.

The Details
- Level **Grades K–4**
- C–P–A **Pictorial, Abstract**
- When to Use It **Warm-Up, Conclusion, Homework, Assessment**
- Time to Allow **5–10 minutes**

Plan Ahead

Each player needs a set of 0–9 digit cards.

Connections to the Common Core State Standards

Content Clusters

Content from any cluster grades K–4 in domains Counting and Cardinality, Operations and Algebraic Thinking, and Number and Operations in Base Ten may be used.

Math Practices

MP2 Reason abstractly and quantitatively.
MP6 Attend to precision.

4 Silent Math

How to Lead the Game

1 Begin by saying that this is a silent game and there will be no talking while playing. You and the players will use only gestures. Aahhh, silence—a thing of beauty!

2 Model how you will show the signs for operations and equals:

- Addition—pointer fingers crossed to show a plus sign

- Subtraction—single horizontal pointer finger as a minus sign

- Multiplication—arms crossed in an X; using arms instead of fingers helps students distinguish between the addition sign and the multiplication sign.

- Division—horizontal pointer finger of one hand with pointer finger and thumb of the other hand above and below it

- Equals—two horizontal pointer fingers held parallel (I've also shrugged my shoulders as if to say "And the answer is . . . ?")

3 Once you've demonstrated the operations, show players how to indicate place value in their answers. For example, for 13 they would show a group of 10 fingers and then 3 fingers, *not* 1 finger and then 3 fingers. For 23 they would show two flashes of 10 fingers (alternating fronts and backs of hands) and then 3 fingers. This makes it easy for you to check their answers.

4 If a player's answer is correct, give him a double thumbs-up. If it's wrong, or if you need the player to show an answer again for whatever reason, wiggle your thumbs up and down to show that a do-over is needed. Do not give a double thumbs-down. Who wants that?

5 Play continues until the players lose interest, you lose interest, your arms get tired from gesturing, or you run out of time.

4 Silent Math

Why This One?

Students get an opportunity to use the four operations to solve basic equations or strings of number sentences. You use fingers and gestures to represent the numbers and operation symbols in an equation. Your students then use mental math to solve the equation and show their answers with their own fingers.

 ## Differentiate It!

Give players a series of tasks with a variety of operations mixed in. This is a string of operations; don't worry about following the order of operations.

Include a variable (or variables) in an equation. Make up and teach a hand signal for that variable before starting to play.

Use two hands vertically, one above the other, to represent fractions. Have players add and subtract, or multiply and divide, basic fractions.

Limit equations to simple operations within your students' ability level— for example, sums to 10 or products with factors between 1 and 5.

Instead of having players show their solutions with their fingers, let them build the solution with manipulatives.

Allow players to "phone a friend" for support by pointing to a friend with one hand and holding their other hand up to an ear to signal a phone call. The friend shows the player the answer, but the player requesting support must still show you the answer.

 ## Tips from the Trenches!

- This is a great game for days when students are wound up and you need a quiet, purposeful activity. Isn't that every day? Use it to promote a quiet environment at the beginning of a lesson. It's also a great filler for five minutes at the end of the day or while waiting for a transition.

- When the answers get so large that players are flashing groups of 10 like crazy, you may want to shift to an individual response format. That way, you can do some assessing and not lose your mind.

The Details

- Level **Grades K–5**
- C–P–A **Pictorial, Abstract**
- When to Use It **Warm-Up, Conclusion, Assessment**
- Time to Allow **5–10 minutes**

Plan Ahead

No preparation needed, but allow extra time to teach the gestures the first time you play.

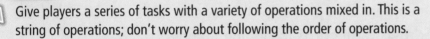

Connections to the Common Core State Standards

Content Clusters

K.OA.A Understand addition as putting together and adding to, and understand subtraction as taking apart and taking from.

1.OA.D Work with addition and subtraction equations.

2.NBT.B Use place value understanding and properties of operations to add and subtract.

3.OA.C Multiply and divide within 100.

4.NF.B Build fractions from unit fractions by applying and extending previous understandings of operations on whole numbers.

5.NF.B Apply and extend previous understandings of multiplication and division to multiply and divide fractions.

Math Practices

MP2 Reason abstractly and quantitatively.
MP6 Attend to precision.

5 Roll High, Roll Low

Objective

Use the digits rolled to make the highest- and lowest-value numbers.

Materials

10-sided die or set of 0–9 digit cards

Directions

Read directions to student players as needed.

1 Find out how many place values to play with. Draw a chart on lined paper. Make one column for each place value needed, plus one out box.

2 Start with Roll High. The goal is to make the highest possible number. One player or the teacher rolls the 10-sided die or draws digit cards to get the numbers.

- One number is rolled or drawn at a time. Choose where to write each number *before* the next roll.

- The same digit may be rolled or drawn more than once.

- Only one number may go in the out box.

- When the Roll High row is full, including the out box, compare results. The player with the highest number wins the round. There may be more than one winner.

3 One player or the teacher rolls or draws numbers for Roll Low. Zero may go in the highest place-value position. Whoever has the lowest number wins the round. See if there is an even lower number using the same digits.

4 Whoever wins the most rounds wins the game.

Sample Chart Heads

TASK	Thousands	Hundreds	Tens	Ones		Out Box
Roll High						
Roll Low						

5 Roll High, Roll Low

Why This One?

Roll High, Roll Low helps students reinforce and extend place value understanding and competency while having fun. The leader (you or a student) rolls a 10-sided die or draws digit cards to generate digits. Players choose the best location for each digit to create the number of either greatest or least value.

 ## Differentiate It!

Have players write each digit for both Roll High and Roll Low at the same time, on the same roll.

Have players write the numbers they make in expanded form.

Have players round their numbers to a specific place.

Play the game with decimal fractions. In the chart, include a decimal point and a box for a whole number before it as well as an out box for an unwanted digit.

Have players label each box in the chart with the appropriate place-value term.

Give players place-value materials to help them build their numbers.

 ## Tips *from the* Trenches!

- Watch your precious cherubs, as they may try to wait to place their digits until they know the next few rolls. That's cheating!

- In my class, it got to the point where I could draw an up arrow, a down arrow, and the number of place values on the board, and the kids would make their charts as they settled in. We were quickly "ready to roll" (pun intended).

- As an assessment, give students a few tasks to do. For example, ask them to increase the largest number by 10, round the smallest to the nearest 100, and write three numbers that fall between the two new numbers. Collect for grading.

The Details
- Level **Grades 1–5**
- C–P–A **Abstract**
- When to Use It **Warm-Up, Conclusion, Review, Assessment**
- Time to Allow **10–20 minutes**

Plan Ahead

You need a 10-sided die or a set of 0–9 digit cards.

Connections to the **Common Core State Standards**

Content Clusters
1.NBT.B, 2.NBT.A Understand place value.
3.NBT.A, 4.NBT.B Use place value understanding and properties of operations to perform multi-digit arithmetic.
4.NBT.A Generalize place value understanding for multi-digit whole numbers.
5.NBT.A Understand the place value system.
5.NBT.B Perform operations with multi-digit whole numbers and with decimals to hundredths.

Math Practices
MP2 Reason abstractly and quantitatively.
MP6 Attend to precision.

6 Math Sports

How to Lead the Game

1 Choose a sport and make its field or court on a board, interactive whiteboard, or chart paper. For example, for baseball you'll need a diamond with four bases. You can use any sport that appeals to your students—basketball, football, hockey, lacrosse—as long as you know it well enough to make its field or court.

2 Arrange players in two teams facing each other in rows of chairs. Each team has one "player on the field" (a paper cutout or sticky note). Explain that players will solve problems to move the player in whatever way works for the game—for example, around the bases for baseball or to the end zone for football.

3 Call up the first player in each row to solve a problem or give a math fact. The first player to do so correctly gets to advance her team's player on the field. All the players move one chair up the row so that two new players are up.

4 Play continues until time runs out or a predetermined score is reached.

Tips for Playing

• For word problems, set a timer for a few minutes while each team works together on a team solution. The first team with the correct solution gets to move its player on the field. If neither team solves the problem in time, reset the timer or post a new problem.

• Mark certain problems with sports connections, such as "A correct answer is worth a home run" or "A correct answer gains 30 yards."

6 Math Sports

Why This One?

Many students love competitive sports such as baseball and football. Sports-related games are a great entry point for them to work on any math concept you need to review, from basic number recognition to comparing, to rounding, to finding the sum of angles or the unknown in an algebraic equation.

 Differentiate It!

As team members approach the board to play, provide more challenging questions for those who are ready for them.

Make sure the strongest players go head-to-head with each other. Have some extra-challenging problems on hand for those pairings.

Provide word problems for teams to solve. If a multi-step problem is answered correctly, advance in a manner that reflects the problem—for example, move two bases on a baseball field if a two-step problem is solved correctly.

Allow players to solve problems in pairs or even as a whole team.

Encourage players to use manipulatives and other math tools to help them solve the problems presented. This is helpful for simple challenges, such as building the equation represented in a number sentence, and for more complex tasks, such as solving a word problem.

 **Tips** *from the* **Trenches!**

- As you arrange players in their seats, optimize the pairing opportunities so that those who are similarly skilled with the concept play against each other.

- Encourage players to come up with a team name, do team chants, and share team strategies.

- If you have an interactive whiteboard, use it to create a field, players, and a roster. If you run out of time before the game is over, you can save the game and quickly pull it up to complete at a later time.

The Details

- Level **Grades 1–5**
- C–P–A **Concrete, Pictorial, Abstract**
- When to Use It **Warm-Up, Lesson, Conclusion, Intervention / Extension**
- Time to Allow **20–30 minutes**

Plan Ahead

Choose the sport to use and prepare its field or court.

Prepare a list of questions for the game. You can use flash cards, problems from a book or website, or come up with your own.

Connections to the Common Core State Standards

Content Clusters
1.OA.C, 2.OA.B Add and subtract within 20.
3.OA.C Multiply and divide within 100.
4.NBT.A Generalize place value understanding for multi-digit whole numbers.
5.NBT.A Understand the place value system.

Math Practices
MP6 Attend to precision.

7 Number Mastermind

Objective

Guess the mystery number in the fewest tries.

Materials

Paper & pencil or board to make chart

Directions

1 Each player creates a chart with three columns: "Guess," "How Many Correct Digits?," and "How Many Digits in Correct Place?"

2 The leader (teacher or partner) chooses a mystery number between 00 and 99. If the mystery number is less than 10, then 0 is the first digit of the number.

3 Players guess numbers. For each guess, the leader says how many digits are correct and how many digits are in the correct place.

4 Players keep track of the leader's answers in their charts and use the information to figure out the mystery number.

Example

If the mystery number is 28:

- Guess is 25: 1 digit correct, 1 digit in correct place
- Guess is 23: 1 digit correct, 1 digit in correct place
- Guess is 82: 2 digits correct, 0 digits in correct place
- And so forth until the mystery number is guessed.

Guess	How Many Correct Digits?	How Many Digits in Correct Place?

7 Number Mastermind

Why This One?

This game is a fun, quick way to get students to think logically, look for patterns in numbers, and recognize the importance of place in the value of a digit. It is extremely low prep and can be done as a class using either one class chart or individual charts made by students.

Differentiate It!

Change the number range to 000 to 999 or even 0,000 to 9,999.

Have players write their guesses in expanded form. This supports place-value understanding.

After a series of successful guesses, have players critique the guesses. What makes a good guess? How did a particular guess build on earlier ones? How did another guess miss an opportunity? Players can then explain their critiques in writing.

Write or post the available digits in a visible area while players are guessing. To help players see which digits are still available and which are not, remove each digit once it's been ruled out by guessing.

Each time a digit is eliminated, review how the clues from the guesses show that the digit is not part of the mystery number.

Tips *from the* **Trenches!**

- The mystery number should be a mystery only to the players, not to you! Write it down, because sometimes it's hard to remember.

- Once players understand the premise, this can be a fun game to play with a partner while waiting for others to finish their work or as an extension activity.

The Details
- Level **Grades 2 & 4**
- C–P–A **Abstract**
- When to Use It **Warm-Up, Conclusion**
- Time to Allow **5–10 minutes**

Plan Ahead

Choose whether to use a class chart or individual charts.

Connections to the Common Core State Standards

Content Clusters
2.NBT.A Understand place value.
4.NBT.A Generalize place value understanding for multi-digit whole numbers.

Math Practices
MP3 Construct viable arguments and critique the reasoning of others.
MP7 Look for and make use of structure.

8 Mile a Minute

How to Lead the Game

1 Divide the class into pairs in whatever way you choose. One student in each pair becomes Player 1, and the other becomes Player 2.

2 Explain that Player 1 will face a list of 10 vocabulary words, while Player 2 faces away. Identify where the word list will be and have players face toward or away from the spot.

3 Post the list where all the Player 1s can see it. When time starts, Player 1 gives verbal clues, uses gestures, or describes a context to convey the meaning of each word to Player 2. As soon as Player 2 guesses the correct word, Player 1 starts giving clues for the next word.

4 Players have one minute to get through the entire list. If a pair completes the list before time is up, have them celebrate silently with a wave of their hands.

5 When the first round is done, partners switch places and Player 2 gives Player 1 clues for the second list of words.

More Game Rules

- Player 1 *may not* use rhyming words. For example, if the word is *square*, Player 1 may not say "Sounds like hair."

- Player 1 *may* make connections to the real world. For example, if the word is *parallel*, Player 1 may say "Like a set of train tracks."

- If Player 2 is struggling, Player 1 may say "Skip" and move on to the next word. The players can go back to any skipped words if time remains.

8 Mile a Minute

Why This One?

This is a quick, engaging game to get students to play with the words they've been learning and studying in mathematics. I have yet to hear of off-task players; all players are engaged because the game is short and to the point. You can play it any time you need to review vocabulary.

 Differentiate It!

Provide a longer list of words but the same amount of time.

Use a vocabulary list that draws from more than one content cluster.

Arrange the word list in order from most difficult word to least difficult word to encourage students to work through the difficult vocabulary words while they're fresh.

Let Player 2 see the word list, too (using a different order), then choose the correct word by listening to the clues from Player 1.

Provide pictorial support for the vocabulary words, or allow Player 1 the option of drawing picture clues for Player 2.

Use one word at a time instead of the full list and play as a whole group, with the entire class trying to get one player to say the word.

 **Tips** *from the* **Trenches!**

- Make lists within a given category—for example, "words we learned while measuring angles," "types of polygons," or "words associated with multiplication."

- At the start of the year, use this game to review vocabulary from previous years.

- This game works well for vocabulary practice and review, but not to introduce new terms.

The Details
- Level **Grades 2–5**
- C–P–A **Abstract**
- When to Use It **Warm-Up, Conclusion**
- Time to Allow **5–10 minutes**

Plan Ahead

You need a timer.

Prepare 2 lists of vocabulary words that students know (10 words each).

Prepare to post the word lists where players can see them.

Connections to the Common Core State Standards

Content Clusters
Content from any cluster grades 2 to 5 may be used.

Math Practices
MP5 Use appropriate tools strategically.

9 Solve!

How to Lead the Game

1 Players stand in a circle. Explain that the players, as a group, will spell a math word, then define that word. Play a round or two for practice until they get the hang of it.

2 Say a math word for the group. The first player says the word.

3 The next player says the first letter of the word, the following player says the next letter, and so on until the word is spelled. If a player says the wrong letter or no letter, she is out and the next player tries.

4 The next player after the word is spelled correctly says the word and gives the definition. If the player gives an incorrect definition, he is out and the next player says the word and gives the definition.

5 The next player after the correct definition is given says, "Solve!" You can use another word if you prefer. Try the school mascot's name or the title of the math unit being reviewed (for example, Graphing!).

6 The next player after "Solve!" is out, just for being the next player.

7 Play continues with the other words on the list until only one player is left standing. That player wins.

9 Solve!

Why This One?

Math vocabulary needs practice. Words such as *addend* or *hexagon* are not often heard outside of math class. Some words, like *factor*, have different meanings outside of math. Solve! is a fun way to practice math vocabulary. There's a little bit of spelling practice, some review of definitions, and the luck of the draw to keep it fun—because some players will be out just because of where they are standing.

 ## Differentiate It!

In addition to having players give the definition of the vocabulary word, require them to use the word in a sentence that provides a cross-curricular connection or real-world application.

Choose academic vocabulary words that are cross-curricular and difficult to describe and define but are important in math—for example, words such as *justify*, *explain*, *acute*, and *difference*.

Provide players with a small write-on whiteboard and erasable marker to record each letter of the word as it is said aloud during the spelling phase.

Post a list of all the vocabulary words with their definitions where all the players can see it.

 ## Tips *from the* Trenches!

- Modeling this game is imperative to its success. Once players get the concept, it works smoothly and effectively. Those first few rounds will be a little bumpy, but stick with it, because it's fun!

- To reduce distractions and keep the game moving, have players arrange their chairs in a circle instead of standing in a circle that keeps shrinking. Players sit down when they're out and stand up at the start of a new game.

The Details

- Level **Grades 2–5**
- C–P–A **Abstract**
- When to Use It **Warm-Up, Conclusion**
- Time to Allow **15–30 minutes**

Plan Ahead

Prepare a list of familiar vocabulary words that need reviewing.

Connections to the
Common Core State Standards

Content Clusters
Content from any cluster grades 2 to 5 may be used.

Math Practices
MP6 Attend to precision.

10 BACON

How to Lead the Game

1 Have players write B-A-C-O-N on a sheet of paper, with room to write numbers under each letter, as in the chart below.

2 Explain that the game has five rounds, one for each letter in the word. Each round has many rolls of the die. Players mentally add up the rolls. The goal is to get the highest sum for each round. At any time during any round, a player may choose to sit down, record his sum as the score for that round, and stop. Why would a player do that? If the BACON number is rolled, any player still standing gets 0 for that round.

3 Roll the die to determine the BACON number. For example, if you roll a 4, then 4 is the BACON number for all five rounds of the first game.

4 All the players stand at the start of each round. Roll the die for the B round (the first round). Roll it again and remind the players to mentally add the two numbers together. (You should keep track of the sum, too!) Roll it again and have the players mentally add that roll to the previous sum. If a player chooses to sit down, she needs to say "Down" so you can monitor who is sitting and who is left standing.

5 Continue to roll the die until all the players have decided to record their scores or until the BACON number is rolled. This can take a while in the early days of playing BACON. However, as most players learn the game, they'll sit down sooner.

6 All players stand up at the start of the next round. At the end of five rounds, players total their scores. The greatest sum wins.

B	A	C	O	N

10 BACON

Why This One?

BACON gives players a competitive, interactive, and physical way to work on number sense and fluency in mental addition. BACON also encourages logical decision making, because in each round players must choose whether to stop playing and keep their score, or keep playing and risk a score of 0.

 Differentiate It!

Put players in groups and have them work with their final sums: arrange their sums from least to greatest, round each sum to the nearest 10 or 100, mentally find the sum of all their sums, or do another task you give them.

Have players create new rules or criteria for the game. Let them play again, then have them discuss how their modifications changed the game.

For each roll, give players ideas for mental math calculations by saying things such as "Let's make that a 10 and add the 1s," "We know the double of that number," or "Let's increase that number by 10 and subtract 1." Suggestions like these support the mental math strategies you're teaching in class.

Have players record scores for each round as tallies instead of numerals. Focus on groups of 5 and groups of 10.

 **Tips** *from the* **Trenches!**

- Model a round or two so players see what it looks like to stay standing and accumulating a score, or to sit down and record a score before the end of the round.

- It can be tempting to use a 10-sided die to get larger numbers for mental math. However, the BACON number is less likely to come up, and it can take too long to have all the players sitting. Stick with a regular die and keep the pace moving!

- Even with a 6-sided die, players can get lucky and stay standing for a long time. Ask those few players to agree to all sit at the same time to keep the game moving. This happens rarely, but it's nice to have an exit strategy.

The Details

- Level **Grades 3–4**
- C–P–A **Abstract**
- When to Use It **Warm-Up, Conclusion**
- Time to Allow **20–30 minutes**

Plan Ahead

You need 1 die.

Connections to the Common Core State Standards

Content Clusters
3.NBT.A, 4.NBT.B Use place value understanding and properties of operations to perform multi-digit arithmetic.

Math Practices
MP2 Reason abstractly and quantitatively.
MP6 Attend to precision.
MP8 Look for and express regularity in repeated reasoning.

11 Roll 5 to 205

Objective

Estimate, add, and get as close as possible to 205 without going over.

Materials

Two dice, paper & pencil

Directions

1   Make a scorecard like the one below, using lined paper. The space at the bottom is for the total.

2   Listen for the numbers rolled by the leader. Quickly decide which number to write in the tens place on the scorecard and which to write in the ones place. For example, if the leader calls out a 3 and a 2, write either 32 or 23.

3   The leader rolls four more times. Write the numbers on the scorecard, as before. After each roll, estimate in your head the total of the numbers already written down, then write down the estimate. The goal is to get as close as possible to a total of 205 without going over.

4   At the end of the five rolls, add up all the numbers. The player who gets closest to 205 without going over wins.

5   Play another game and see if you can get closer to 205.

Roll 5 to 205 Scorecard

Tens	Ones

11 Roll 5 to 205

Why This One?

Estimating and rounding are essential life skills. These skills are also expected as part of the Common Core State Standards. This game is a fun way to practice estimating and rounding.

Differentiate It!

Change the scorecard to include a decimal point and one more place value: __ . __ __ (ones, decimal point, tenths, hundredths). Instead of 5 to 205, use a range of 0.5 to 20.5.

Have players form small groups. At the conclusion of the game, have all the group members add up the differences between their estimates and totals. The group with the smallest sum wins.

Instead of 5 to 205, use a range of 50 to 2005. Roll three dice instead of two.

Allow more time between rolls so players have more time to think about their choices.

Let players check their estimates by doing some quick addition on paper before the next roll.

Tips *from the* Trenches!

- This is meant to be a fast-paced game of quick estimating, rounding, and computing. Keep up the pace and encourage quick decision making. Play lots of quick games so that estimation becomes second nature.

- For a fun atmosphere roll two large dice, roll the dice under a document camera, or roll big virtual dice on an interactive whiteboard so players can see what you've rolled in addition to hearing it.

The Details
- Level **Grades 3–4**
- C–P–A **Abstract**
- When to Use It **Warm-Up, Conclusion**
- Time to Allow **5–10 minutes**

Plan Ahead

You need 2 dice and a way to show the rolls to all the players.

Connections to the Common Core State Standards

Content Clusters
3.NBT.A Use place value understanding and properties of operations to perform multi-digit arithmetic.
4.NBT.A Generalize place value understanding for multi-digit whole numbers.

Math Practices
MP2 Reason abstractly and quantitatively.
MP6 Attend to precision.

12 Roll Up to 100

Objective

Add numbers to get as close as possible to 100 or another number without going over.

Materials

6- or 10-sided die

Directions

1 On lined paper, make a chart like the one below. Make seven rows for seven rolls.

2 Find out the target number (100 or another number). Write it at the top of the chart.

3 Roll the die or listen for the leader's roll. Write the number rolled in the chart. Decide how to multiply the number—by either 1 or 10. Write the answer in the box under ×1 or ×10. Write it again under Running Total.

4 Roll again or listen for the second roll. Decide how to multiply, and record your answer. Then choose to either add or subtract this number from the running total and write the answer in that column.

5 Keep playing through all seven rolls. The final total should not go over the target number. After seven rolls, the player with the number closest to the target wins.

Other ways to play: Start at 100 and roll down to 0. Use 1,000 as the target and multiply by 1, 10, or 100. Use a target number that ends in something other than 0. Use dollar amounts. Multiply by 5, 10, 15, or 20.

Target Number: _____

Roll	Number Rolled	×1	×10	Running Total
1				
2				
3				

12 Roll Up to 100

Why This One?

This fun logic game supports multiplying by 10 or 100, as well as adding and subtracting. Players like the challenge of getting close to the target number without going over. They like seeing how different people making different choices can end up with different answers, even though they start with the same numbers. You can vary the game by subtracting while rolling down from 100, by changing the target number, or by changing the numbers used to multiply each roll.

 ## Differentiate It!

Increase the target to 1,000 or 10,000. Add options for multiplying by 1, 10, or 100, or 10, 100, or 1,000 to the chart.

Use a dollar amount as the target to incorporate decimals to hundredths.

Have players write their totals on sticky notes and use them to create a class bar graph on chart paper. This reinforces Content Clusters 4.MD.B and 5.MD.B, Represent and interpret data.

Change the column headings to multiply by factors such as 4, 7, and 8 to have players practice those difficult-to-master math facts.

Let players use manipulatives on a place-value mat to model groups of 1 and 10 for each roll. Have them regroup the manipulatives to model the running total.

Tips *from the* Trenches!

- Another way to win: If players go multiple rounds, have them find the difference between their answers and the target number for each round. Add the differences from all rounds; the player with the lowest sum wins.

- Here's a good rule that a favorite mentor taught me: "Don't do for students what they can do for themselves." It's okay to give players the model chart to copy the first few times. After they understand the game, let them come up with their own ways to organize the numbers for each roll.

The Details
- Level **Grades 3–5**
- C–P–A **Abstract**
- When to Use It **Warm-Up, Lesson, Assessment**
- Time to Allow **10–20 minutes**

Plan Ahead

You need a 6- or 10-sided die.

Connections to the Common Core State Standards

Content Clusters

3.NBT.A Use place value understanding and properties of operations to perform multi-digit arithmetic.

4.NBT.A Generalize place value understanding for multi-digit whole numbers.

5.NBT.B Perform operations with multi-digit whole numbers and with decimals to hundredths.

Math Practices

MP6 Attend to precision.
MP8 Look for and express regularity in repeated reasoning.

13 Math Practices Dice Roll

How to Lead the Game

1 Choose a meaningful problem or performance task—something the players can really dig into. Share the Math Practices Dice Roll Prompts (page 111) with all players.

2 At the beginning of the task, roll the die. Read aloud the before-task prompt that goes with the number you rolled.

3 Ask players to respond to the prompt either orally or in writing.

- If they respond orally, have them turn to a partner to share their thinking *before* they get started on the task. This allows for an "oral rehearsal." Players may choose to modify their approach to the task before they solve the problem.

- If they respond in writing, this is a great opportunity to collect their responses so you can gauge their thinking.

4 Allow time for students to work on the task.

5 At the conclusion of the task, roll the die again and read aloud the after-task prompt that goes with the number you rolled. Allow time for either oral or written responses.

13 Math Practices Dice Roll

Why This One?

The Common Core State Standards include the expectation that students will talk and think about math. The question always is, "How do I get them to do this?" With this game, you choose any math task or story problem, then roll a die to come up with a prompt to get players thinking and talking. The before-task prompts in the copymaster are designed to help players utilize one or more of the Mathematical Practices to get started on a problem, to persevere, or to explain their thinking. At the end of the problem, you roll again for an after-task prompt; these prompts help players reflect on the process. Over time, this way of doing business will become habitual; students will approach problems by thinking about them first and making a plan of attack, even without rolling any dice.

Differentiate It!

Increase the rigor of the problems.

Require answers to include at least one piece of supporting evidence.

For students who need additional support, model, model, model math discussion before asking players to reflect independently. Gradually release responsibility for responses to the players.

Provide a cloze passage for players to fill in before and after the problem. You may need to prepare these passages in advance so that you're ready for any prompt that is rolled.

Tips *from the* Trenches!

- Be explicit about the Mathematical Practices students are using. Each prompt on page 111 lists associated practices. Post a copy of the practices where students can see it, and read the associated practices aloud after reading the prompt.

- Use the before-and-after prompts to assess both students' understanding of the content and their use and understanding of the Mathematical Practices.

The Details
- Level **Grades 3–5**
- C–P–A **Abstract**
- When to Use It **Warm-Up, Lesson, Conclusion, Homework, Assessment**
- Time to Allow **5–10 minutes**

Plan Ahead

You need 1 die, Math Practices Dice Roll Prompts (page 111), and a worthwhile problem or task that requires more than basic computation.

Decide how to share the prompts with your students—for example, make copies or display them with a document camera.

Connections to the Common Core State Standards

Content Clusters
Content from any cluster grades 3 to 5 may be used.

Math Practices
Any of the eight practices may be addressed, depending on the roll of the die.

14 Roll a Question

Objective
Talk or write about math.

Materials
30-sided die or number cards 1–30

Directions

Do a math problem. Roll the die. Use the prompt with the number rolled to begin a discussion about the problem you just solved.

1 Why did you choose that method to solve the problem?

2 How did you get that answer?

3 Describe what is the same and/or different about two solutions.

4 How did you know which operation(s) to use?

5 Explain what _____ means. (Teacher fills in the blank.)

6 Why is that your answer?

7 Prove that your answer is correct.

8 Could you use another strategy? If yes, what? If no, why not?

9 Have you seen a problem like this before? How was it similar?

10 What's your reasoning for solving the problem that way?

11 Agree or disagree with a classmate's reasoning about the problem.

12 FREE CHOICE from prompts 1 to 11.

13 Add to a classmate's ideas about the math problem.

14 Why did you do your work that way?

15 Is there another way to solve the problem? What is it?

16 Finish this sentence: "_____ (A classmate's) solution reminds me of . . ."

17 If you solved the problem again, what would you do the same? What would you do differently?

18 What vocabulary did you need to know?

19 What was the most difficult part? The least difficult part?

20 What was your first step? Why?

21 How does this problem connect to the real world?

22 What math standards does this problem go with?

23 How can you check your work? Think of two ways.

24 In a sentence, describe the problem you solved.

25 What key pieces of information did you need?

26 Write a problem similar to the one you solved. Solve it.

27 What math skills did you need to solve the problem?

28 FREE CHOICE from prompts 13 to 27.

29 What conclusions can you draw?

30 What observations can you make?

14 Roll a Question

Why This One?

Getting a class conversation started usually isn't an issue; it's keeping the discussion focused on math. This game helps. After students have completed a math task, such as a math story problem or constructed response, you randomly choose a number from 1 to 30, then use that numbered prompt from the copymaster on the facing page to start the discussion.

Differentiate It!

Ask players to choose and discuss several questions instead of just one.

Ask players to write their own "top 10" lists of discussion questions.

Craft a shorter list of questions for players to choose from.

Model how to answer questions before giving students so many options. For example, model how to respond to one of the discussion questions, then practice discussing that question as a class. Later, introduce another discussion question, model how to use it for discussion, and practice it.

Tips *from the* Trenches!

- You can start out by choosing a question for the entire class to talk about. Once students have seen how it's done, they can choose partners, then each pair can roll the die or pick a card and have their own short math conversation. That provides a bit more freedom.

- If you plan to do this multiple times, give students copies of the list to paste in their math journals, or hand out clear plastic sleeves to hold the lists. You know some students will lose them if you don't!

The Details

- Level **Grades 3–5**
- C–P–A **Abstract**
- When to Use It **Warm-Up, Lesson, Conclusion, Homework, Assessment**
- Time to Allow **5–15 minutes**

Plan Ahead

You need a 30-sided die or cards with numerals 1–30.

Decide how you will provide the questions to all players.

Connections to the **Common Core State Standards**

Content Clusters
Content from any cluster grades 3 to 5 may be used.

Math Practices
MP3 Construct viable arguments and critique the reasoning of others.

15 Six-Number Equations

Objective

Use the 4 operations on 5 numbers to come up with the 6th number as the answer.

Materials

Paper & pencil

Directions

1 Use any method to choose five random numbers between 0 and 25. Don't use 0 or 25. Write the numbers down to remember them.

2 Choose a sixth random number. Write an equal sign. Write the sixth number to the right of the equal sign.

3 Use the five numbers and +, −, ×, and ÷ to come up with an equation that equals the sixth number. The equation should look like the lines below, with a number on each line and an operation (+, −, ×, or ÷) between the numbers.

___   ___   ___   ___   ___ = ___

For example, $5 + 2 + 11 ÷ 3 + 6 = 12$

More Game Rules

• Each number may be used only once.

• The sixth number rolled must be the answer. The other five numbers may be arranged in any order.

• Any of the four operations (+, −, ×, and ÷) may be used as many times as necessary.

• Show all work and do not erase solutions that don't work out. Circle any correct solutions and check them for accuracy.

• Work for 10 to 15 minutes, then stop even if you do not have a correct solution yet. Look over your attempts and think about them.

15 Six-Number Equations

Why This One?

This game gives students a way to "mess with the math," emphasizing process over results. It allows multiple entry points for students, honors the process of manipulating numbers, provides practice for all four operations, and gives students a way to persevere in computations.

 Differentiate It!

When a player comes up with a viable solution, let him know he is not finished. Acknowledge the solution, then ask, "Is there another way?" Or have the player justify an answer by asking, "How do you know you are correct?"

Ask players to come up with equations that work when they correctly follow the order of operations while solving. Have them record the equation properly.

Have players use only even numbers in the blanks to provide numbers that are easier and more comfortable to work with.

Limit the choices to numbers less than 15 and designate a number that students are familiar with working toward, such as 10, for the solution.

Tips *from the* **Trenches!**

- Try using a classroom "Stumped" bulletin board. If your class has an unsolved problem, it goes on the Stumped board for anyone to work on during a few spare minutes. If you have a set of six numbers with no solution by the end of the time you have available to play, honor that unsolved problem by posting it on your Stumped board.

- A student's unsuccessful attempts provide you with a formative assessment opportunity for glimpsing how he is approaching the problem. It may also be worthwhile to record the amount of time a student spends "messing with the math," including how many attempts he makes while persevering and how many solutions he finds.

The Details

- Level **Grades 4–5**
- C–P–A **Abstract**
- When to Use It **Warm-Up, Conclusion, Homework, Extension, Assessment**
- Time to Allow **15–30 minutes**

Plan Ahead

Decide how players will choose random numbers.

Connections to the Common Core State Standards

Content Clusters
4.NBT.B Use place value understanding and properties of operations to perform multi-digit arithmetic.
5.NBT.B Perform operations with multi-digit whole numbers and with decimals to hundredths.

Math Practices
MP1 Make sense of problems and persevere in solving them.
MP3 Construct viable arguments and critique the reasoning of others.
MP6 Attend to precision.

16 Tens Go Fish

Objective

Using 2 cards, create combinations that total 10.

Materials

Deck of cards with face cards removed

Directions

Read directions to student players as needed.

1 One player deals five cards to each player. The dealer places the rest of the cards in the middle as the "pond." In this game, an ace equals 1.

2 Players look at their cards. If any combinations add up to 10, or if a player has a 10 card, they place the card(s) faceup on the table. Then they draw cards from the pond to replace the cards laid down.

3 The player to the right of the dealer asks another player for a specific card that will complete a 10 with a card in her hand. For example, if the player has a 3, she asks another player for a 7 to make a sum of 10.

4 If the player who was asked does not have the card, he says, "Go fish," and the player who asked draws a card from the pond.

5 The next player takes a turn.

6 The game ends when no more cards are left in the pond or when no one can make another combination of 10. The winner is the player with the most combinations of 10.

16 Tens Go Fish

Why This One?

This game provides practice with facts to 10 by upping the expectations on the time-tested game "go fish." Instead of asking for cards with matching numbers, a player asks for a card that sums to 10 when added to a card in his hand.

 Differentiate It!

Have players count their total groups of 10 and keep score—for example, "I have 7 groups of 10, so my score is 70."

Have students play with more than one deck and require them to use two or three cards to create sums to 20.

Have players make combinations that total 100 by choosing cards for the tens and ones places. For example, if a player had a 2 and a 7, that could represent 27, and the player would then ask the other players for a 7 and a 3 to represent 73.

Tell students to play with more than one deck to create more opportunities for combinations of 10.

For students who may be confused by the additional symbols on a playing card, make special card decks in which the number of symbols matches the numeral on each card.

For more pictorial support, have students play with 10-frame cards rather than traditional playing cards.

Tips *from the* **Trenches!**

Sometimes accountability is an issue with games. Don't let it be! To promote accountability, have players record their various combinations that make 10. Collect their recording sheets at the end of the game.

The Details

- Level **Grades K–2**
- C–P–A **Pictorial, Abstract**
- When to Use It **Review, Homework, Intervention / Extension**
- Time to Allow **15–20 minutes**

Plan Ahead

Each pair or group needs a deck of cards with the face cards removed.

Connections to the Common Core State Standards

Content Clusters

K.OA.A Understand addition as putting together and adding to, and understand subtraction as taking apart and taking from.
1.OA.C, 2.OA.B Add and subtract within 20.

Math Practices

MP2 Reason abstractly and quantitatively.
MP6 Attend to precision.

17 Stoplight

Objective

Get to 100 or another target number before the other players.

Materials

10-frame; 10 dice, each with 3 green sides, 2 yellow sides, and 1 red side

Directions

Read directions to student players as needed.

1 Players take turns. Player 1 rolls all 10 dice. If any dice land green side up, he keeps going. If not, his turn is over.

2 Player 1 places any green-side-up dice on a 10-frame grid for score. Each die equals 1 point. Then he decides if he wants to keep the score he has or roll the remaining dice again. What to do if Player 1 rolls again:

- If any more dice land green side up, add them to the 10-frame grid. Score 1 point for each die added.

- If all dice land red side up, the turn ends with a score of 0.

- If no dice land green side up, some dice land red side up, and some land yellow side up, pause to decide whether to stop and keep the score or keep rolling.

- Once the score is recorded, the player removes all the dice from the 10-frame grid.

3 Play continues around the circle. After each turn, the player adds up her scores from all her turns so far. The first player to reach or pass 100 wins.

Game Strategies

- A player may stop rolling at any time and record the score for that turn. Her turn is over, and her score is safe.

- A player may keep rolling as long as green or yellow sides keep coming up.

- In most cases the highest possible score for each turn is 10, because there are 10 dice and each green die scores 1 point. But if a player rolls green for all 10 dice during one turn, she may roll again to try to score more than 10 for that turn.

17 Stoplight

Why This One?

Rolling multiple dice is exciting in and of itself. When you add stoplight colors and players making decisions about keeping their scores or risk trying for more, you've got a winning combination to work on sums to 10, as well as counting and adding within 100.

 Differentiate It!

Make each die worth 10 rather than 1 and roll to 1,000 instead of 100.

For students who are ready for multiplication, transition from this game to Greedy (page 82).

Ask students to record each of their rolls and show all of their work as mathematical equations, rather than just giving the total for each roll.

Have players tally the score from each roll and circle the groups of 10 in their cumulative scores.

Provide a hundred chart and small objects as markers to help players track their progress toward 100.

 **Tips** *from the* **Trenches!**

- If you have blank dice, use either permanent markers or colored sticky dots to turn them into stoplight dice. Colored sticky dots work on regular dice, too.

- Printable 10-frame templates are easy to find on the Web.

- Help players make the connection to a stoplight: green means keep going, yellow means slow down and decide, and red means stop.

- Emphasize number bonds of 10. Encourage players to see that they are making 10s as they add dice to the 10-frame grid.

The Details

- Level **Grades K–3**
- C–P–A **Concrete, Pictorial, Abstract**
- When to Use It **Lesson, Review, Intervention / Extension**
- Time to Allow **15–20 minutes**

Plan Ahead

Each pair or group needs a blank 10-frame grid and 10 dice marked with 3 green sides, 2 yellow sides, and 1 red side.

Connections to the **Common Core State Standards**

Content Clusters
K.CC.A Know number names and the count sequence.
1.NBT.A Extend the counting sequence.
2.NBT.A Understand place value.
3.NBT.A Use place value understanding and properties of operations to perform multi-digit arithmetic.

Math Practices
MP2 Reason abstractly and quantitatively.
MP8 Look for and express regularity in repeated reasoning.

18 Oh, Darn!

Objective

Be the first player to reach 100 without going over.

Materials

Two dice

Directions

Read directions to student players as needed.

1 Player 1 rolls the dice. If she rolls a 1 on one of the dice, then her turn ends and her score is 0. If not, she adds the two numbers in her head.

2 Player 1 may keep rolling and adding to the total in her head. But if she rolls a 1, her turn is over and her score for that turn is 0, no matter how many points she's added in her head so far on that turn.

3 When Player 1's turn is over, Player 2 takes a turn, and so on.

4 On each player's next turn, the new rolls are added to her score from her earlier turn(s).

5 The first player to reach exactly 100 wins. If you go over 100, you lose.

More Game Rules

- A player may stop rolling at any time, end his turn, and record the score.

- If a player rolls *two* 1s, the player's *total* score from all his turns goes back to 0.

- When a player reaches a score of 94, two rules change: the player may roll one die instead of two dice, and rolling a 1 simply scores 1 point—it no longer ends the turn and cancels the score.

18 Oh, Darn!

Why This One?

The element of chance in this game and the all-or-nothing nature of rolling a 1 makes Oh, Darn! a classroom favorite. Players find sums as they try to be the first to reach 100 without losing their points from a turn, or even losing their total cumulative score.

 Differentiate It!

Have students play to 1,000 instead of 100. Each roll of the die is worth 10 times the rolled number. For example, if a 2 is rolled, it counts as 20.

Have players try different strategies and explain the outcomes. For example, what happens if they always stop after one turn and record their score? What happens if they always go for it and keep rolling?

Have players keep track of the number of times in each game that a 1 is rolled or that two 1s are rolled. Look at the data for any patterns, then test any guesses about the patterns they notice.

Let players use manipulatives on place-value mats so they can more easily understand the addition they are doing.

Have players move a marker on a hundred chart to model the addition as they are mentally adding the numbers rolled.

 **Tips** *from the* **Trenches!**

- Take on the entire class and try to beat them to 100. Students decide as a class if they'd like to keep rolling or bank their current score. Of course everyone must agree on what the current score is, after adding it mentally.

- Divide your class into two large groups that play against each other, making group decisions, while you facilitate the rolling and record keeping.

- Using either of these two variations, play six rounds, one for each letter in the game's name, OH, DARN! After one side rolls a 1 and scores 0, that side receives a letter. When one side has spelled OH, DARN, the game is over. This approach makes a longer game with more chances to modify strategies.

The Details
- Level **Grades K–3**
- C–P–A **Abstract**
- When to Use It
  **Warm-Up,
  Conclusion,
  Homework**
- Time to Allow
  10–20 minutes

Plan Ahead

Each pair needs 2 dice.

**Connections to the
Common Core
State Standards**

Content Clusters
K.OA.A Understand addition as putting together and adding to, and understand subtraction as taking apart and taking from.
1.NBT.C, 2.NBT.B Use place value understanding and properties of operations to add and subtract.
3.NBT.A Use place value understanding and properties of operations to perform multi-digit arithmetic.

Math Practices
MP2 Reason abstractly and quantitatively.
MP6 Attend to precision.
MP8 Look for and express regularity in repeated reasoning.

19 Face-Off

Objective

Collect the most cards.

Materials

Deck of cards with face cards removed

Directions

Read directions to student players as needed.

1 Find out from the teacher what rule to follow for the game. For example, should each partner play one card and partners compare numbers? Or should each partner play two cards and compare the sums, differences, or products of those two numbers? Or use the two cards to create fractions to compare?

2 Divide the deck so each player has the same number of cards.

3 Play the first round. Whoever has the card or the answer with the greater value takes all the cards. An ace equals 1.

4 If there's a tie, have a face-off. Each player deals three cards facedown and one card faceup (or two cards faceup if playing that way). The player with the highest value from the faceup cards takes all the cards on the table. If the faceup cards have the same value, deal more cards for a double face-off.

5 Play continues until one player has all the cards, or until time's up. The player with all or most of the cards wins.

19 Face-Off

Why This One?

You may know this oldie but goodie as "war" or "snap." Regardless of your students' content needs, this game can work for you. Young players can play by the standard rules: deal one card each and compare the values. Older players deal two cards, then do the operation of your choice: add, subtract, multiply, or turn into a fraction. Whoever has the greater answer wins that round.

 ## Differentiate It!

Have players deal three cards on each round and either add all three addends or multiply all three factors.

Make cards that go up to 20 for students who are working on fluency with larger numbers.

Challenge capable students to subtract any red cards and add any black cards. You may go as far as designating red cards as negative integers and black cards as positive integers, then explaining how to use the value of integers to add, subtract, and multiply.

Create custom card sets for student pairs who may need additional support. For example, make 10-frame cards or numeral cards that each show the same number of objects as the numeral on the card. (Standard playing cards show more objects than the numerals indicate.)

Work on operations introduced at an earlier grade level.

 ## Tips *from the* Trenches!

Pair students who need to work on the same skills. For example, pair two students who need to work with math facts to 10, two who are ready for all addition and subtraction facts within 20, two who are working on multiplication facts, and so forth.

The Details

- Level **Grades K–5**
- C–P–A **Concrete, Pictorial, Abstract**
- When to Use It **Review, Homework, Intervention / Extension, Assessment**
- Time to Allow **15–20 minutes**

Plan Ahead

Each pair needs a deck of cards with the face cards removed.

As needed, make custom cards for student pairs. See Differentiate It!

 Connections to the **Common Core State Standards**

Content Clusters
K.CC.C Compare numbers.
1.OA.C, 2.OA.B Add and subtract within 20.
3.OA.C Multiply and divide within 100.
4.NF.A Extend understanding of fraction equivalence and ordering.
5.NF.A Use equivalent fractions as a strategy to add and subtract fractions.

Math Practices
MP2 Reason abstractly and quantitatively.
MP6 Attend to precision.

20 Sneak Peek

Objective

Be the player with the lowest total score.

Materials

Deck of cards

Lay out cards like this.

No Peeking

Peeking Okay

Directions

Read directions to student players as needed.

1 Each player makes a scorecard as shown below.

2 One player deals four cards to each player, facedown. The dealer places the remaining cards in a draw pile.

3 Each player lays his cards in two rows of two. Players may peek at cards in the bottom row, but not in the top row. The goal is to have the lowest score. Cards are scored: queen = 0, ace = 1, king = 2, jack = 10, and number card = face value.

4 Players take turns drawing. A player may discard a drawn card or trade it for any of his four cards, placing it face-down. Discarded cards go faceup in the pile.

5 The next player may draw from the new card pile or the discard pile.

6 When a player thinks his score is the lowest of all the players' scores, he knocks on his next turn instead of drawing a card. All the players turn over their cards and add up their scores for the round. If the knocker's score is the lowest, all the players keep their scores. If the knocker's score is not the lowest, his score becomes the total of all the scores for the round; the other players keep their scores. The round ends.

7 The player with the lowest total score after nine rounds wins.

Sneak Peek Scorecard

Round	1	2	3	4	5	6	7	8	9	Total
Score										

20 Sneak Peek

Why This One?

This game provides a context for addition and subtraction within 20 and also creates opportunities to use logical reasoning. Students may decide to keep playing, or they may use logic to decide whether they should conclude their round and find their sum. It's ideal for practicing cluster content in grades 1 and 2, but all grades and ages love to play this game—their strategies increase along with their age.

Differentiate It!

Make the game more complex by telling players to subtract the values of red number cards and add the values of black number cards. Do not get into numbers with negative values unless you are challenging students in the upper elementary grades.

Make the consequence for knocking and not having the lowest score more severe. For example, the player who knocks gets the sum of all the players' scores (including her own), while the other players score 0 for that round instead of scoring their card values.

Allow players to peek at all four cards.

Have players use manipulatives to represent and keep track of their scores. Have players hide their manipulatives behind a screen so other players cannot see their scores.

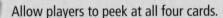

Tips *from the* Trenches!

Playing a demonstration round—on an interactive whiteboard, under a document camera, or gathered around a table—is a good way to demonstrate how peeking and knocking work. Call for a few student volunteers to play with you, lay out the cards, and show which cards are okay to peek at. Knock to end the round, whether or not you have the lowest score, and demonstrate what happens next. Once students have the hang of it, have them play in pairs or small groups.

The Details

- Level **Grades 1–2**
- C–P–A **Abstract**
- When to Use It
  Review, Intervention / Extension
- Time to Allow
  15–20 minutes

Plan Ahead

Each pair or group needs a full deck of cards.

Connections to the Common Core State Standards

Content Clusters
1.OA.C, 2.OA.B Add and subtract within 20.

Math Practices
MP2 Reason abstractly and quantitatively.
MP6 Attend to precision.
MP7 Look for and make use of structure.

21 Exact-O-Mo

Objective

Be the first player to reach the exact total of 20 without going over.

Materials

Deck of cards with face cards removed

Directions

Read directions to student players as needed.

1 Players divide the cards evenly between themselves. They do not look at their cards until they play them.

2 Player 1 turns over his first card. Player 2 turns over her first card, then says a number sentence that adds the two cards together. Ace equals 1. For example, if Player 1 turns over a 5 and Player 2 turns over an Ace, Player 2 says, "5 plus 1 equals 6."

3 Player 1 turns over another card and says a number sentence that adds the new card to the total. Using the same example, if Player 1 turns over a 3, he says, "6 plus 3 equals 9."

4 Play continues until the sum of 20 has been reached. If the sum goes over 20, the player subtracts the next card instead of adding it. For example, if the sum is 24 and a 6 comes up next, the player says, "24 minus 6 equals 18."

5 The player who turns over the card that results in the exact sum of 20 wins the round. The player who wins the most rounds by the time the game ends is the winner.

21 Exact-O-Mo

Why This One?

This game is a fantastic way to get students to manipulate numbers using both addition and subtraction within 20. Players develop fluency while they're having some fun. You can even use up those incomplete card decks—a win-win situation!

 Differentiate It!

Choose a target number that is greater than 20.

Include face cards and give each face card a value—for example, jack = 11, queen = 12, and king = 13.

For older students who are ready for positive and negative integers, have the red cards represent negative numbers and the black cards represent positive numbers. Have players try to reach a total of 0.

Put several decks together and remove the higher-number cards. That way, players are working with smaller addends more frequently.

Allow players to use a number line or hundred chart as a scaffold for adding and subtracting.

Have players model their number sentences on a place-value mat using base-10 blocks or place-value disks. If players are working below 100, you'll need a chart with only ones and tens.

 **Tips** *from the* **Trenches!**

- This game is best played with homogeneous pairings.

- Require players to state the addition or subtraction number sentence so the other players can check their work.

- At the end of the school year, gather together any partial or incomplete card decks and save them for playing Exact-O-Mo next year. You don't need a complete deck for this game, and you can use any number of partial decks combined to create one game deck.

The Details

- Level **Grades 1–2**
- C–P–A **Abstract**
- When to Use It **Review, Intervention / Extension**
- Time to Allow **10–20 minutes**

Plan Ahead

Each pair needs a deck of cards with the face cards removed. Decks may be incomplete.

Connections to the **Common Core State Standards**

Content Clusters
1.OA.C, 2.OA.B Add and subtract within 20.

Math Practices
MP6 Attend to precision.

22 Tic-Tac-Ten

Objective

Be first to finish a row that sums to 10 in any direction.

Materials

One die, paper & pencil

Directions

Read directions to student players as needed.

1 One player draws a tic-tac-toe board.

2 Player 1 rolls the die and writes his rolled number somewhere on the board.

3 Player 2 rolls the die and writes her rolled number somewhere on the board. Keep in mind that the goal is to get three numbers in a row that total 10.

4 Player 1 rolls again and writes his next number on the board. Player 1 may write the number to complete a row that sums to 10 and win the game. Player 1 may instead write the number where it will block Player 2.

5 Play continues until one player completes a sum of 10 using three numbers, or until there is a tie game, with all the boxes filled but no sum of 10.

6 Players may keep playing for a certain number of games or as long as time allows. They can use tally marks to keep track of how many games each player wins.

22 Tic-Tac-Ten

Why This One?

The game of tic-tac-toe is quick and easy. Why not use it to make practicing facts to 10 quick and easy, too? This game is super-low prep yet gives students a quick way to develop that coveted fact fluency within 10.

Differentiate It!

Have students try playing Tic-Tac-Hundred. They roll two dice for each turn, decide which number to use for tens and which for hundreds, and write the numbers in the grid so that three numbers in a row—horizontally, vertically, or diagonally—make a sum of 100.

Have students create a graph to represent a series of games. Graphs can show wins, losses, and ties for each player. Have students write about their graphs: do they observe any patterns in the results?

Before having students play this game with numbers, review the rules of traditional tic-tac-toe by playing with Xs and Os. Then transition to the game using numbers with the goal of adding to 10. Encourage players to look for similarities and differences between the two versions of the game.

Let players use a number line or manipulatives to support their addition.

Tips *from the* Trenches!

- Tie games happen a lot when playing regular tic-tac-toe with Xs and Os. Make sure players are prepared for ties during this version of the game, too. You may want to explain why one player may choose to block the other player and force a tie by writing a number in a space, even when doing so will not result in a winning sum to 10.

- Have students draw several tic-tac-toe boards in their math journals or notebooks so they can jump right into the game when they have a few spare minutes. They can record whom they played and who won next to each game board.

The Details

- Level **Grades 1–2**
- C–P–A **Abstract**
- When to Use It **Warm-Up, Conclusion, Homework**
- Time to Allow **5–10 minutes**

Plan Ahead

Each pair needs 1 die.

Connections to the **Common Core State Standards**

Content Clusters
1.OA.C, 2.OA.B Add and subtract within 20.

Math Practices
MP2 Reason abstractly and quantitatively.
MP6 Attend to precision.

23 Stink Eye

Objective

Have the largest grand total after 6 games.

Materials

Two dice, one with a stink eye side; Stink Eye Scorecard (page 112) for each player

Directions

Read directions to student players as needed.

1 Player 1 rolls the dice. If a stink eye comes up on the first roll, she rolls again. (A stink eye is not counted on the first roll.)

2 Player 1 records the two numbers under "Game 1, Roll 1" on her scorecard. Then she either adds or multiplies the numbers—whichever she's practicing—and writes the answer to complete a number sentence. For example, if she rolls a 6 and a 4 and she's practicing addition, she would write 6 + 4 = 10. For multiplication, she would write 6 × 4 = 24.

3 Player 1 then decides if she wants to play it safe or risk getting a stink eye.

- To play it safe, she records the answer to the number sentence as her Game 1 total.

- To try for a higher score, she rolls again. If no stink eye is rolled, she writes the next number sentence and answers it. If a stink eye is rolled, she scores 0 for Game 1.

- The player may roll up to four times in each game. If no stink eye comes up, her game total is the sum of all four answers.

4 When Player 1's turn is done, Player 2 takes a turn. Play continues until the players have completed six games.

5 Each player adds the total scores from all six games. The player with the highest grand total wins.

23 Stink Eye

Why This One?

Who doesn't like a little risk when it's all in fun? In this game, players make choices about taking risks while working on fluency with either addition or multiplication facts. They have multiple rounds to play and in the end it's the grand total that decides the winner, so there's always a chance to risk it all or risk nothing!

 Differentiate It!

Create dice for students who are ready to practice multiplication facts for higher numbers. Write the factors 7, 8, 9, 11, and 12 on two blank 6-sided dice. Instead of marking a 10, use that side for the stink eye. Multiples of 10 are easy, and don't need as much practice!

Have players double their totals after completing the initial operation (addition or multiplication).

Provide a number line to support counting or skip counting while adding or multiplying.

Create dice that include only addends that sum to no more than 10 or factors that produce products less than 60.

Have students play fewer games so they have fewer scores to add up when they are finished.

 Tips *from the* Trenches!

For this game, it's best to pair students who are about equally fluent. To facilitate this, color-code the dice and hand them out according to students' level of fact fluency. When choosing a partner, a student with a green die, for example, must find another student with a green die to play with. Make sure that one player in each pair has a stink eye on his die.

The Details

- Level **Grades 1–3**
- C–P–A **Pictorial, Abstract**
- When to Use It **Review, Homework, Intervention / Extension**
- Time to Allow **15–25 minutes**

Plan Ahead

Each pair or group needs 2 dice. Cover the 1-dot side of one die in each pair with a sticky dot to make a stink eye.

Each player needs a copy of Stink Eye Scorecard (page 112).

Connections to the **Common Core State Standards**

Content Clusters
1.OA.C, 2.OA.B Add and subtract within 20.
3.OA.C Multiply and divide within 100.

Math Practices
MP2 Reason abstractly and quantitatively.
MP6 Attend to precision.

24 Sum Target

Objective

Be the first player to reach the target by adding numbers.

Materials

Two different kinds or colors of playing pieces

Directions

Read directions to student players as needed.

1 Players choose a target number between 25 and 55.

2 Players take turns placing their pieces on the game board (below) and adding the numbers they claimed. Each time a player puts down a piece, she says the current total and the new total. For example, if the current total is 21 and she puts a piece on a 5, she says, "21 plus 5 equals 26."

3 The first player to reach the target number wins.

4 Play continues for as many rounds as time allows. Players choose a new target number for each round.

Game Board

5	5	5	5	5
4	4	4	4	4
3	3	3	3	3
2	2	2	2	2
1	1	1	1	1

24 Sum Target

Why This One?

Number and Operations in Base Ten is a big domain in elementary school, because it's imperative for students to master the ability to manipulate numbers fluently at this level. This game gives students lots of practice "messing" with addition using various combinations of numbers.

 Differentiate It!

Change the numbers on the game board to include decimals to the hundredths and change the range of the available target numbers to match. For example, have players choose a number between 4 and 10 and use decimal values from 0.10 to 0.55 on the game board.

Have students create their own version of the game specifically designed to help them challenge themselves and their peers on various topics from their grade level's cluster content.

Have players build their current totals using manipulatives such as place-value disks on a place-value mat.

Have players track their addition using a hundred chart.

 **Tips** *from the* **Trenches!**

For variety, have players try different strategies to see what happens. For example, players could work their way up from the bottom of one column or alternate going up and down columns. Or one player could choose only odd numbers, and another player could choose only even numbers to see what happens. As they do this, have them look for patterns in the play—who wins, who loses, and why. After trying a variety of strategies, players can write about what they noticed and explain any patterns they observed.

The Details

- Level **Grades 1–3**
- C–P–A **Concrete, Abstract**
- When to Use It **Review, Homework, Intervention / Extension**
- Time to Allow **10–15 minutes**

Plan Ahead

Each pair needs a copy of the game directions and 2 different kinds of objects (or colors of objects) to use as playing pieces.

Connections to the Common Core State Standards

Content Clusters
1.NBT.C, 2.NBT.B Use place value understanding and properties of operations to add and subtract.
3.NBT.A Use place value understanding and properties of operations to perform multi-digit arithmetic.

Math Practices
MP2 Reason abstractly and quantitatively.
MP3 Construct viable arguments and critique the reasoning of others.
MP6 Attend to precision.

25 Ninety-Eight

Objective

Be the last player in the game without going over 98.

Materials

Deck of cards, Ninety-Eight Card Values (page 113)

Directions

1 Players review the value or action of the cards, listed in the card values chart.

2 One player deals five cards to each player and places the rest in a draw pile.

3 The oldest player lays down a card and then draws a card from the pile. Play continues to that player's left (clockwise).

4 The next player adds a card to the first card and says the equation. For example, if Player 1 lays down a 6 and Player 2 lays down a 5, Player 2 says, "6 plus 5 equals 11."

5 Each player plays a card and draws a card on each turn. The player looks at the chart to see how each card played affects the total and the way the game is played.

6 When the total reaches 98, players may use only one of these cards: a 3 card to reverse direction of play, a 4 card to add 0, or a 10 card to subtract 10. The total may not go over 98.

7 If a player has only cards that would bring the total over 98, that player is out. The other players keep playing.

8 The last player left when everyone else is out wins.

25 Ninety-Eight

Why This One?

This game has fun, complicated rules that allow students to think about game strategy while practicing addition and subtraction to 100. As time goes on, students develop strategic plans for playing and saving cards that help them emerge as the winner—the final player holding cards at the end.

 Differentiate It!

Have players subtract the value of red number cards, unless another rule supersedes doing so. For example, 4 is always 0 regardless of color, but a red 8 subtracts 8, while a black 8 adds 8.

As players learn the rules, have them add their own. For example, players could add the rule that playing a 2 doubles the current score; if 24 is the current total and a 2 is played, the score becomes 48.

Provide a hundred chart as a scaffold for adding and subtracting.

For player reference, supplement the Ninety-Eight Card Values copymaster with a large anchor chart that shows only the card names and what they do. This helps keep the game moving, because players who read slowly don't need to read the card value explanations on the copymaster.

 **Tips** *from the* **Trenches!**

- You can choose to display the card values where all the players can see them or make a copy for each group of four.

- Although the suggested range for this game is grades 2 to 4, I've played this game with first graders to 77-year-olds. It's a fun, "on your toes" kind of game that works great for a buddy class to play with younger students. The older the players, the more strategy they use; the younger the players, the more they focus on operations.

The Details

- Level **Grades 2–4**
- C–P–A **Concrete, Pictorial, Abstract**
- When to Use It **Review, Homework, Intervention / Extension**
- Time to Allow **20–30 Minutes**

Plan Ahead

Each group needs a deck of cards and Ninety-Eight Card Values (page 113). Card values sheet may be posted or copied and handed out.

Connections to the **Common Core State Standards**

Content Clusters
2.NBT.B Use place value understanding and properties of operations to add and subtract
3.NBT.A, 4.NBT.B Use place value understanding and properties of operations to perform multi-digit arithmetic.

Math Practices
MP2 Reason abstractly and quantitatively.
MP6 Attend to precision.
MP7 Look for and make use of structure.

26 Four in a Row

Objective

Be the first player to mark 4 products in a row.

Materials

Four in a Row Game Board (page 114), 2 paper clips, 2 kinds of playing pieces

Directions

1 Player 1 places paper clips over two factors in the row above the game board. These are the two factors to start with.

2 On the game board, Player 1 covers the product of those two factors with one of her playing pieces.

3 Player 2 may move *one* paper clip to a different factor. He then covers the product of those two factors with one of his playing pieces.

4 Player 1 may move *one* paper clip to a different factor on her next turn.

5 Play continues until one player has marked a line of four products in a row horizontally, diagonally, or vertically.

More Game Rules

- One player may try to block the opposing player.

- Both paper clips may be placed on the same factor. On the next move, only one paper clip may be moved.

- Players may not move a playing piece once it has been placed on the board. They may place one playing piece on top of another, blocking the opposing player from making four in a row.

26 Four in a Row

Why This One?

Timed math tests don't always engage students, but kids still need to develop fluency with multiplication facts. This game allows students to develop fact fluency and adds a little strategy, too!

Differentiate It!

↪ Challenge players to try for five in a row.

↪ Change the game board and factors to practice skills related to decimals, fractions, or another more advanced concept.

↪ Practice addition facts: use the numbers 0 to 9 as addends and change the game board to show possible sums instead of possible products.

↪ Limit play to the first five factors (using only the first three or four rows) and give players manipulatives so they have the opportunity to build their products. Encourage them to arrange manipulatives in arrays using the two factors as length and width.

↪ Allow players to skip count on a number line to find the product of the two factors.

Tips *from the* Trenches!

This game makes great homework. Students can teach the game to a parent, guardian, or sibling, who may welcome the chance to play a game to practice multiplication facts rather than using flash cards or timed tests. If no one at home is available to play, kids may play with a stuffed animal. Show them how to take turns back and forth with their toy, playing both sides for twice the fun!

The Details

- Level **Grade 3**
- C–P–A **Abstract**
- When to Use It **Review, Homework, Intervention / Extension**
- Time to Allow **15–20 minutes**

Plan Ahead

Each pair needs a copy of Four in a Row Game Board (page 114), 2 paper clips, and 2 kinds of playing pieces (pennies & dimes, 2 colors of bingo chips, 2 kinds of beans).

Connections to the **Common Core State Standards**

Content Clusters
3.OA.C Multiply and divide within 100.

Math Practices
MP2 Reason abstractly and quantitatively.
MP6 Attend to precision.

27 Block It

Objective

Cover the most total area on the chart.

Materials

Two dice, 2 colors of writing tools, pencil, 1-centimeter graph paper

Directions

1 The players choose different colors of writing tools.

2 Player 1 rolls two dice and decides how to use the two numbers for length and width. Then he uses his color to outline an array (rectangle) on the paper.

3 Player 1 colors in the array then, inside the array, writes and solves the equation for its area (length × width = area). Write the equation and solution in pencil.

4 Player 2 rolls two dice and decides which number to use for length and which for width, for an array.

5 Player 2 outlines an array somewhere else on the same sheet of paper using her color. She colors in the array and writes the equation.

6 As the game continues, less and less space is available. Players have to think strategically to place their arrays.

7 When neither player can make an array, each player totals his area values (products). The player with the most total area covered wins.

Block It Sample

$2 \times 2 = 4$

$2 \times 3 = 6$

$1 \times 5 = 5$

27 Block It

Why This One?

This game is a practical way for students to use multiplication facts to create arrays, to practice the concept of area, and to apply reasoning to think strategically. Your spatial thinkers will love this game and they'll be adding up their total area before your very eyes, using the products of their rolls.

 ## Differentiate It!

Give players paper with smaller units, such as quarter-inch graph paper. This makes the game last longer and provides more opportunities for larger arrays (products) and more strategic thinking.

Allow players to roll the dice twice and add two numbers together to get greater lengths and widths.

Allow students to manipulate their arrays, but only if doing so creates the same area. For example, if a 4 × 8 array is rolled, allow students to place a 16 × 2. The product remains the same as their roll, and they choose the array's shape by the best placement opportunity available on the board.

Encourage players to use manipulatives, such as Cuisenaire rods, to lay out their arrays. That way, they can understand the array concretely, not just pictorially.

Allow players to use a multiplication chart to help solve the equations. This puts the focus on area rather than multiplication.

 ## Tips *from the* Trenches!

Sometimes just changing the equipment can make an old game new and enticing again. If you have access to dice within dice, have players roll one of these instead of two regular dice. The inner die determines length, and the outer die determines width.

The Details

- Level **Grades 3–4**
- C–P–A **Pictorial, Abstract**
- When to Use It
  **Lesson,
  Review,
  Homework,
  Intervention / Extension**
- Time to Allow
  15–20 minutes

Plan Ahead

Each pair needs 2 dice, 2 writing tools in different colors, and a sheet of 1-centimeter graph paper.

Connections to the Common Core State Standards

Content Clusters
3.MD.C Geometric measurement: understand concepts of area and relate area to multiplication and to addition.
4.MD.A Solve problems involving measurement and conversion of measurements from a larger unit to a smaller unit.

Math Practices
MP2 Reason abstractly and quantitatively.
MP7 Look for and make use of structure.

28 Tangling with Angles

Objective

Accumulate the smallest difference between estimates and measurements of angles.

Materials

Protractor, ruler, paper & pencil

Directions

1 Both players make scorecards like the one shown below.

2 Player 1 uses a ruler to draw an angle on a sheet of paper.

3 Player 2 names the angle (acute, right, or obtuse), estimates its measurement, and records both on his scorecard.

4 Player 1 uses the protractor to measure the angle. Both players check the measurement and agree on its precision. Player 2 records the measurement on his scorecard, then subtracts to find the difference between the estimate and the measurement. This is Player 2's score.

5 The players trade roles; Player 1 now names the angle, estimates, and scores. Player 2 first draws and later measures the angle.

6 After a certain number of rounds, the players add up their scores. The player with the lowest total score (the smallest difference between his estimates and the actual measurements) wins the game.

Tangling with Angles Scorecard

Round	Name of Angle	Estimate	Actual	Score
1				
2				
3				

28 Tangling with Angles

Why This One?

This game is an easy and fun way to practice everything to do with angles. Players first create scorecards, then play in pairs to draw angles, name them, estimate their measurements, measure them, and find the difference between each estimate and actual measurement. The player with the most accurate estimates wins.

Differentiate It!

Have Player 1 draw two angles. Player 2 gives an estimate of the sum of both angles, in addition to naming both angles and estimating their individual measurements.

Have students estimate the degree measurement to complete a right angle or complete circle.

Provide players with a reference sheet giving angle names, pictures of sample angles, and corresponding measurement ranges.

Provide different protractors for angles within a given range. For example, mark one protractor for acute angles only (1° to 89°) and another for obtuse angles (91° to 179°).

Tips *from the* Trenches!

- Before playing the game, review how to use a protractor. Do not use this game to teach this skill, however.

- Players may struggle if angles are drawn "too short" to reach the numbers on a protractor. Demonstrate how to use a ruler to extend the rays.

- Model ways to remember angle names. Use your arms and sayings such as "acute = ah, cute!" and "right = just right."

- Make sure to draw right angles facing both ways. Often we present right angles as facing right, and students don't learn that what makes a right angle a right angle is the fact that it measures 90°, not that it faces right.

The Details

- Level **Grade 4**
- C–P–A **Pictorial, Abstract**
- When to Use It **Lesson, Homework, Intervention / Extension, Assessment**
- Time to Allow **20–30 minutes**

Plan Ahead

Each pair needs a protractor, a ruler, and paper & pencil.

Connections to the **Common Core State Standards**

Content Clusters
4.MD.C Geometric measurement: understand concepts of angle and measure angles.
4.G.A Draw and identify lines and angles, and classify shapes by properties of their lines and angles.

Math Practices
MP4 Model with mathematics.
MP5 Use appropriate tools strategically.
MP6 Attend to precision.

29 Greedy

Objective

Be first to score 10,000 points.

Materials

Six dice

Directions

1 Each player rolls once to start. The player with the highest roll gets to go first. Play continues to the player's left.

2 A player rolls all six dice. The player must roll a 1, a 5, or a combination listed in the score chart (below) to score and continue. The player sets aside any dice that are scored. The player may roll the remaining dice again to add to the score for that turn, or the player may choose to end the turn.

3 If a player rolls the remaining dice and does not roll a 1, a 5, or a combination from the score chart, his turn is over, and no scores from that turn are counted—not even scores from the first roll.

4 If a player scores all six dice on one roll, he may choose to roll again using all of the dice and add any new score to his total.

5 When a player reaches or passes 10,000 points, each of the other players gets one more turn to try for 10,000. The player with highest score at the end of the final round wins.

Score Chart

1 = 100	Three 2s = 200	Four of any number other than 1 = 1,200
5 = 50	Three 3s = 300	Five of any number other than 1 = 2,000
Three 1s = 1,000	Three 4s = 400	1, 2, 3, 4, 5, 6 in one roll = 2,000
Four 1s = 2,000	Three 5s = 500	Six of any number = The Game!
Five 1s = 2,500	Three 6s = 600	

29 Greedy

Why This One?

The competitive nature of this game keeps players engaged while practicing multiples of 100 and 1,000. Players must think strategically about how to score each roll. They must also choose whether to stop rolling and keep a score, or continue rolling and risk losing that turn's score by being too greedy. Players practice addition by keeping a running total of their scores from all their turns.

 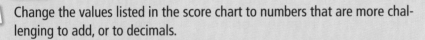

Differentiate It!

Change the values listed in the score chart to numbers that are more challenging to add, or to decimals.

Add in a value for a "full house" (three of one number and two of another). Rolling a full house leaves one die to roll again, if the player chooses to. At that point the player would need to roll either a 5 or a 1 in order to not lose the turn.

Have pairs of students play against other pairs, with each pair making joint decisions. This approach requires players to justify their choices and holds each accountable to another player.

Reduce the values listed in the score chart to multiples of 10 and 100 and score to a maximum of 1,000 points. For example, instead of "1 = 100 (points)," have "1 = 10." Instead of "Five 1s = 2,500," have "Five 1s = 250."

Tips *from the* **Trenches!**

At first glance, this game may seem too complex for some students to understand. Modeling it as a fishbowl task helps everyone to know what to do. Post the score chart where everyone can see it, then play with a group of students in the center of the room while the others observe. Afterward, each student who played with you becomes an "expert" in one of the new pairs or groups.

The Details

- Level **Grades 3–5**
- C–P–A **Abstract**
- When to Use It
  **Review,
  Intervention / Extension**
- Time to Allow
  20–30 minutes

Plan Ahead

Each pair or group needs 6 dice.

Connections to the Common Core State Standards

Content Clusters
3.NBT.A Use place value understanding and properties of operations to perform multi-digit arithmetic.
4.NBT.A Generalize place value understanding for multi-digit whole numbers.
5.NBT.A Understand the place value system.

Math Practices
MP2 Reason abstractly and quantitatively.
MP6 Attend to precision.
MP8 Look for and express regularity in repeated reasoning.

30 Par 3

Objective

Have the lowest score after 9 holes.

Materials

Deck of cards with face cards removed; Par 3 Scorecard (page 115) for each player

Directions

1 Par 3 is like a round of golf with nine holes. It's also like a card game because it uses cards. One player is the dealer. The dealer turns up a card for Hole 1. This is the target number for that hole. All the players write the target number on their scorecards.

2 The dealer gives three cards to each player for Hole 1. Each player uses his cards and the four operations (+, –, ×, ÷) to try to create a number sentence with an answer that equals the target number.

• A player who comes up with a number sentence that equals the target using only these three cards receives the best possible score: 0.

• A player may draw up to five more cards to use in the number sentence. However, each additional card is a point added to his score—whether or not he uses the card.

• A player scores the number of cards drawn after the first three, even if the target isn't reached.

3 Each player records his number sentence and solution, if any, as well as his points earned, for Hole 1.

4 The players return the cards to the bottom of the deck. The dealer then turns up a new target number and deals three cards to each player for Hole 2.

5 This pattern is repeated for all nine holes. Reshuffle cards as needed. The player with the lowest score at the end of nine holes wins.

30 Par 3

Why This One?

This game provides a fun and sports-themed way for younger students to "mess with" addition and subtraction and for older students to practice all four operations. Fooling around with math in this way helps students develop fluency and gives them opportunities to notice patterns in numbers. Players can challenge themselves to look for multiple number sentences using the same numbers but different operations.

 ## Differentiate It!

↪ Have players draw more than three cards. All the cards must be included in the number sentence in order to reach par.

↪ Tell players to use red cards as negative numbers and black cards as positive numbers and to add the integers together for each number sentence.

↪ Provide players with squares of paper with the four operations and the equal sign to help them keep track of their number sentences.

↪ Provide players with a number line or multiplication chart for reference as they add, subtract, multiply, and/or divide to get as close as possible to par.

 **Tips** *from the* **Trenches!**

While this game is good at any time, I like to save it for the spring. Players love a new game later in the school year, and it creates excitement about the coming summer. Plus, it connects to the real-life sport of golf and its unusual goal: to get the lowest score, rather than the highest.

The Details

- Level **Grades 3–5**
- C–P–A **Abstract**
- When to Use It **Warm-Up, Homework, Intervention / Extension**
- Time to Allow **15–25 minutes**

Plan Ahead

Each pair or group needs a deck of cards with the face cards removed.

Each player needs a copy of Par 3 Scorecard (page 115).

Be prepared to explain the meaning of the word *par* in golf.

Connections to the **Common Core State Standards**

Content Clusters
Content from any grade 3 to 5 cluster in Operations and Algebraic Thinking or Number and Operations in Base Ten may be used.

Math Practices
MP1 Make sense of problems and persevere in solving them.
MP6 Attend to precision.

31 Contigo

Objective

Mark the most scorable boxes on the game board.

Materials

Contigo Game Board (page 116), 3 dice, 2 kinds of playing pieces

Directions

1 Player 1 rolls the three dice and adds the numbers rolled. He finds the sum on the game board and puts a playing piece on it. This is the first marked box.

2 Player 2 rolls the three dice. She uses these three numbers and the four operations (+, −, ×, ÷) to try to come up with an answer that appears in a box next to, above, or below the first marked box. If she does, she scores 1 point. If not, she scores 0. Either way, she must come up with an answer and use a playing piece to mark the answer on the board—even if that box doesn't score on that turn.

3 Players take turns rolling the dice and marking boxes to accumulate points. They use tally marks to keep score.

4 After eight rounds, the player with the most points wins.

More Game Rules

- On each turn, a player may use more than one operation and may use the same operation more than once.

- A box must share a side (not a corner) with a marked box to count for a score.

- Each shared side counts for 1 point. A box that shares sides with two marked boxes scores 2 points.

- If a player *can* fill a box on his turn, then he *must* fill a box, even if filling it does not count for a score, and even though that creates up to four new sides for his opponent to play against.

31 Contigo

Why This One?

This game allows practice with the four operations, leading into multi-digit numbers in a safe yet challenging way. Players practice addition, subtraction, multiplication, and division while thinking logically about placement and point accumulation.

 Differentiate It!

Have players use four dice so there are more options for coming up with answers. Players do not have to use all four numbers, but they may.

Give players the opportunity to create their own game board using fractions or decimal fractions.

Use blank dice to make a set of dice with the numbers 7 to 12. Players end up working with larger numbers and different possibilities.

Encourage players to focus only on addition and subtraction, or only on multiplication and division. When they are comfortable with the game, let them choose from all four operations in the same game.

 **Tips** *from the* **Trenches!**

- Make sure students with similar ability levels are paired. This creates a comfortable and challenging environment for all players.

- Circulate around the room and check on players as they solve their problems. Ask them to justify their choices and explain their mathematical thinking.

- To use this game as a formative assessment, require players to record their number sentences for each of their eight turns. This adds accountability to the game and shows you which operations a student is most comfortable using.

The Details

- Level **Grades 3–5**
- C–P–A **Abstract**
- When to Use It **Review, Homework, Intervention / Extension**
- Time to Allow **20–30 minutes**

Plan Ahead

Each pair needs a copy of Contigo Game Board (page 116), 3 dice, and 2 kinds of playing pieces (pennies & dimes, 2 colors of bingo chips, 2 kinds of beans).

Connections to the **Common Core State Standards**

Content Clusters
3.NBT.A, 4.NBT.B Use place value understanding and properties of operations to perform multi-digit arithmetic.
5.NBT.B Perform operations with multi-digit whole numbers and with decimals to hundredths.

Math Practices
MP2 Reason abstractly and quantitatively.
MP3 Construct viable arguments and critique the reasoning of others.
MP6 Attend to precision.

32 You Never Lose

Objective

Find sums of 10.

Materials

Deck of cards with 2 suits of number cards (Ace–10) and all 4 suits of face cards

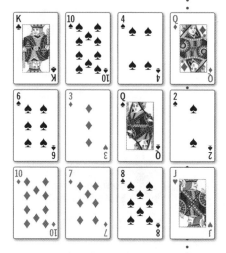

Cover pairs of cards that equal 10 until all the cards are used.

Directions

Read directions to student players as needed.

1 Deal the first 12 cards faceup in a 3 × 4 array, as shown in the illustration.

2 Pick up any face cards (king, queen, jack) and put them on the bottom of the deck. *This is essential!* Replace the face cards with number cards. Keep doing this until only number cards are turned up. In this game, aces equal 1.

3 Now look for any two cards that equal 10. Cover each of them with a card from the top of the deck. For example, 1 (ace) plus 9 equals 10, so cover the ace and the 9 with two other cards. Place the new cards faceup. If you see a 10 card, cover that with another card, too, because 10 plus 0 makes 10. If a face card appears during this part of the game, leave it showing. Do not put it at the bottom of the deck.

4 Keep looking for pairs that equal 10. Cover them with cards from the deck. When you play a face card over another card, that pile is finished. Don't add any more cards to it.

5 If you've played correctly, the array will be all face cards when you draw the last card. You won! If not, the deck may have missing cards. Or maybe you didn't put the face cards on the bottom of the deck, or you chose number pairs that did not add up to 10. Shuffle the cards and give it another go!

32 You Never Lose

Why This One?

Everyone loves a magic trick. This game allows students to work on combinations of 10 while playing a game that feels like a little mathematical magic. Plus, the title is You Never Lose. Doesn't that feel good?

 Differentiate It!

Give a player a stopwatch so he can time himself, starting when the array is ready and stopping when all piles have face cards on top. He can challenge himself to do it faster and faster.

Have players pair off and race against each other, starting when both players have their arrays ready.

Provide players with teacher-made decks of cards in which the number of items matches the numeral on each card. (Standard playing cards show more items than the numerals indicate.) Use blank cards for the 12 face cards or draw a smiley face on each one.

Tips *from the* Trenches!

- Sort out the decks ahead of time. This will preserve your sanity and maximize your students' practice time.

- Save the cards you don't use (two full suits) and use them for other games, such as Exact-O-Mo on pages 66 to 67, or Face-Off on pages 62 to 63.

- For kindergarten, wait to play this game until the end of the year. Teach it to a few students at a time in a small-group setting.

- Make a video of the action while the game is being played (showing only the player's hands) and post it on your website or blog. Send a link to parents so they can see the game in action and help their children play at home.

The Details

- Level **Grades K–2**
- C–P–A **Pictorial, Abstract**
- When to Use It **Warm-Up, Conclusion, Homework, Intervention / Extension**
- Time to Allow **10–15 minutes**

Plan Ahead

Player needs a deck of cards with all 4 suits of face cards, but with 2 suits of number cards removed.

 Connections to the **Common Core State Standards**

Content Clusters
K.OA.A Understand addition as putting together and adding to, and understand subtraction as taking apart and taking from.
1.OA.C, 2.OA.B Add and subtract within 20.

Math Practices
MP6 Attend to precision.
MP8 Look for and express regularity in repeated reasoning.

33 Pyramid Ten

Objective

Use the cards to make bonds of 10 and be left with no pyramid.

Materials

Deck of cards with face cards removed

Directions

Read directions to student players as needed.

1 Lay out 15 cards faceup in a pyramid like the one shown in the illustration: one card at the top, then two cards, three cards, four cards, and five cards at the bottom. The cards should not overlap.

2 Pick up cards in any combination to create bonds of 10. (In this game, an ace equals 1.)

- Begin finding number bonds in the bottom row.

- Do not take a card from the next row up until no more cards in the current row can be used to make a bond of 10.

3 When no more bonds of 10 can be made, fill in the pyramid with cards from the rest of the deck.

4 Keep making bonds of 10 until the pyramid is gone or no more moves are available.

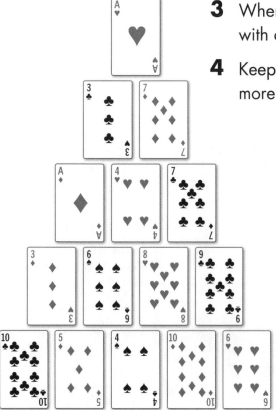

33 Pyramid Ten

Why This One?

Finding bonds of 10 using one, two, and three digits is essential for future mathematical understanding. This solitaire-type game is great for working on this central building block of place value. Students get solo, purposeful repetition in a game-like environment where every pyramid played is similar, but different, depending on how the cards stack up.

 Differentiate It!

Choose a different number bond to challenge players; for example, have them make bonds of 12 or bonds of 16.

Have players write about their observations or the strategies they used to find and build number bonds.

Combine two decks of cards and play to the sum of 20 using one, two, three or more cards to create the sum.

Provide players with teacher-made decks of cards in which the number of items matches the numeral on each card. (Standard playing cards show more objects than the numerals indicate.)

Allow players to build bonds of 10 using manipulatives as they pick up the corresponding cards.

 Tips *from the* Trenches!

Not sure about your students, but my students sometimes misplace cards. Keep all the face cards you remove from the decks and use them to replace missing number cards. Write the missing card's number on the face card in dark marker, or place a sticky note with the new value written on it on the card. That way, all your students will be playing with a full deck—ha-ha!

The Details

- Level **Grades K–2**
- C–P–A **Pictorial, Abstract**
- When to Use It **Warm-Up, Conclusion, Homework, Intervention / Extension**
- Time to Allow **5–10 minutes**

Plan Ahead

Player needs a deck of cards with the face cards removed.

Connections to the **Common Core State Standards**

Content Clusters
K.OA.A Understand addition as putting together and adding to, and understand subtraction as taking apart and taking from.
1.OA.C, 2.OA.B Add and subtract within 20.

Math Practices
MP6 Attend to precision.
MP7 Look for and make use of structure.
MP8 Look for and express regularity in repeated reasoning.

34 Roll, Build, Draw & Write

Objective

Correctly build, draw, and write a number based on its place values.

Materials

One 10-sided die, or 1 set of 0–9 digit cards; objects for building numbers, paper & pencil

Directions

Read directions to student players as needed.

1 Draw a chart like the one shown below, but without the numbers in it. Add as many place values as you are working on—for example, Ones and Tens, or Ones, Tens, and Hundreds.

2 Roll the die twice or draw two cards: the first roll is ones; the second roll is tens; and so forth.

3 Use objects to build the number rolled. For example, if 3 is in the tens place and 2 is in the ones place, use 3 sets of 10 objects and 2 single objects to build 32.

4 Draw a picture of the number you built.

5 Write the expanded form of the number—for example, 30 + 2 = 32.

6 Roll to keep playing. Stop after 10 numbers.

Sample Chart for Ones and Tens

Roll		Draw	Write
Tens	Ones		30 + 2 = 32
3	2	• • • • • • • • • • • • • • • • • • • • • • • • • • • • • • • •	

34 Roll, Build, Draw & Write

Why This One?

This game is a trifecta—a three for one. It incorporates concrete, pictorial, and abstract expectations to get students to compose and decompose numbers according to their place value.

 Differentiate It!

Have players find the sum of all the numbers they built. Let them use their manipulatives or have them add the numerals, depending on their level of understanding.

Have players roll the die more times to generate numbers that have place values into the hundreds or thousands.

Use place-value strips to support players as they write numbers in expanded form.

Require that players only build numbers, or only build and draw them. Omit the abstract components of the game (writing the numeral and its expanded form).

 **Tips** *from the* **Trenches!**

- Finding 10-sided dice can be a challenge. You can give players place-value strips or sets of 0 to 9 digit cards to draw from, or have them make their own digit cards on slips of paper. Anything that allows them to come up with digits at random works for this game.

- Base-10 blocks and place-value disks are nice to have, but any manipulatives will work for building numbers. Consider beans, straws, Popsicle sticks, bingo chips, and so forth. Seeing the number represented in a variety of ways is a good thing!

The Details

- Level **Grades K–2**
- C–P–A **Concrete, Pictorial, Abstract**
- When to Use It **Warm-Up, Lesson, Conclusion, Review, Intervention / Extension, Assessment**
- Time to Allow **10–20 minutes**

Plan Ahead

Player needs a 10-sided die, objects for building numbers such as beans or cold cereal, and paper & pencil.

Connections to the **Common Core State Standards**

Content Clusters
K.NBT.A Work with numbers 11–19 to gain foundations for place value.
1.NBT.B, 2.NBT.A Understand place value.

Math Practices
MP2 Reason abstractly and quantitatively.
MP4 Model with mathematics.
MP6 Attend to precision.

35 To the Top

Objective

Count to the top of the card pyramid.

Materials

Deck of cards with face cards removed

Directions

Read directions to student players as needed.

1 Build a pyramid of cards, placing them faceup. Start with one card at the top, then two cards in the next row. These two cards should overlap the first card. Place three cards in the next row, overlapping the two cards above.

2 Keep going until the pyramid has seven overlapping rows. Hold the rest of the deck in your hands.

3 Turn over the first card in the deck and set it off to the side to start a pile. Using the cards in the pyramid, count up or down from the number on this card. Ace equals 1 in this game.

- Start at the bottom row.

- Pick up the cards as you count them and place them on top of the card off to the side.

- It's okay to count up and down and then up again, for example 3-4-5-6-5-4.

- It's not okay to pick up a card that still has another card overlapping it.

4 If there are no cards to pick up, turn over the next card in the deck, place it on the pile to the side of the pyramid, and begin counting again.

5 Keep going. If you pick up the top card in the pyramid, you win! If there are no cards left in the deck, the game is over. Try again!

35 To the Top

Why This One?

This game is addictive—in a mathematical way. It helps students practice counting up and down from any number 1 to 10. Players also learn to follow simple rules, observe closely, and be nimble in their thinking as they switch between counting up and counting down, as well as moving up and down the rows on the pyramid.

 Differentiate It!

⤹ Leave the face cards in and give each face card a value, such as jack = 11, queen = 12, and king = 13. Have students play the game the same way, but with these additional values.

⤹ Have players find the sum of the cards that are left at the end of the game and keep track of the cumulative total over a number of games. The lower the total of the leftover cards, the better they're doing at the game.

⤷ Tell players to build a pyramid with six rows instead of seven.

⤷ Provide players with, or have players create, a number line so they have a visual reminder of the numbers that come before and after each number they'll be working with.

 **Tips** *from the* **Trenches!**

- Play the game a time or two while your students watch. "Think aloud" as you make each move, so that while students are learning how to play, they can also observe your strategy. If you have a particular plan for uncovering cards to make them available on later turns, the counting up and down can go on for quite a while before you have to turn over a new card from the deck.

- Sometimes the deck and the pyramid are literally stacked against a long run of counting up and down. Encourage players to shuffle all the cards and start over again. The luck of the draw may be with them next time!

The Details

- Level **Grades K–2**
- C–P–A **Pictorial, Abstract**
- When to Use It **Warm-Up, Homework**
- Time to Allow **5–10 minutes**

Plan Ahead

Player needs a deck of cards with the face cards removed.

Connections to the **Common Core State Standards**

Content Clusters
K.CC.A Know number names and the count sequence.
1.NBT.A Extend the counting sequence.
2.NBT.A Understand place value.

Math Practices
MP2 Reason abstractly and quantitatively.
MP6 Attend to precision.
MP7 Look for and make use of structure.

36 OOPS!

How to Set Up the Game

1 On strips of paper or cardboard, or on Popsicle sticks, write problems to help your students practice whatever they need to master. For example, if they're learning to add, write addition problems; if they're comparing fractions, write pairs of fractions to compare. Write the answer on the back of each strip or stick. That way, the problems are self-checking.

2 Write as many problems as you can. For every 10 problems, write the word "OOPS!" instead of a problem.

3 Place all the problems and OOPS! strips or sticks in an opaque container, where players can't see them. An empty tissue box or covered jar works great.

4 Explain to students how to play: Pull out a problem. Solve it. If you get it right, keep it. If you don't, put it back. If you pull out a OOPS!, put all the correct problems back and start again. Play continues until a player runs out of time or tires of the game.

5 Encourage players to keep practicing so they get faster and faster at solving problems and get more and more of the problems correct.

36 OOPS!

Why This One?

This game's versatility is its greatest strength. I love the idea of being able to differentiate the game to meet any student's needs—from basic addition and subtraction facts to using parentheses and brackets to solve equations. After the initial investment of your time (in writing the problems and setting up containers), individual students can play alone, turning any odd moment into math practice.

Differentiate It!

Write some problems with a missing addend, minuend, factor, or divisor instead of a missing solution.

Represent unknowns using a variable such as *x* or *y*.

Make cards or sticks for players to practice comparing written numbers and pictorial representations of the numbers' values.

Let players use tools such as manipulatives, a number line, or a hundred chart to solve the problems.

Tips *from the* Trenches!

- Have each student make an OOPS! container with his name on it. Let students decorate their containers with paper, tape, or stickers. As they master their math skills, change the problems in their OOPS! containers.

- Another way to organize OOPS! containers is by problem type. Have different containers for addition, multiplication, fractions, and other types of problems. Allow anyone in the class to use them.

- To keep skills fresh, put a variety of OOPS! problems in a container for a mixed review. For example, put problems from all four operations, plus some OOPS! cards or sticks, in the same container. This supports ongoing cumulative review—an opportunity to "use it" rather than "lose it."

The Details

- Level **Grades K–5**
- C–P–A **Abstract**
- When to Use It **Warm-Up, Homework, Intervention / Extension**
- Time to Allow **5–10 minutes**

Plan Ahead

Follow the directions on the facing page to prepare problems and containers for this game.

Connections to the **Common Core State Standards**

Content Clusters

K.OA.A Understand addition as putting together and adding to, and understand subtraction as taking apart and taking from.

1.OA.D Work with addition and subtraction equations.

1.OA.C, 2.OA.B Add and subtract within 20.

3.OA.C Multiply and divide within 100.

4.NBT.B Use place value understanding and properties of operations to perform multi-digit arithmetic.

5.OA.A Write and interpret numerical expressions.

Math Practices
MP6 Attend to precision.

37 Elimination

How to Set Up the Game

1 Gather materials for students to make their own sets of geometry cards for the classic matching game concentration. Each student needs 28 cards, markers or crayons, and a rubber band or resealable plastic bag to hold the completed card set.

2 Come up with the content for the 28 cards (14 pairs) to hand out or to post for students to copy by hand. Matching card pairs do not have to be identical. For example, if players are practicing the number of sides in different shapes, a triangle may match with the numeral 3 and a square with the numeral 4. For older students, the terms *right triangle* and *equilateral triangle* might match with pictures of these kinds of triangles.

3 Provide materials to students so they can make their cards.

4 Explain to students how to use the cards. To play alone, the player places the cards facedown in a 4 x 7 array. (Remind students that it helps to keep the rows tidy.) The player tries to find pairs by turning over two cards at a time. If the cards go together, she keeps them. If not, she turns them over again. Players keep going until they have found all the pairs.

5 A student may also play against a classmate who is practicing the same content. Players alternate turning over the cards. The one who picks up the most cards wins.

37 Elimination

Why This One?

Putting a new twist on the old card game concentration helps students practice concepts related to shapes, angles, and their attributes. You determine the card content ahead of time, then have students copy your work by hand to make their own decks. This takes the big prep away from you and puts it in the hands of the students. Plus, when students create their own cards, they gain additional practice and have more ownership of the game.

Differentiate It!

Create card pairs that require some solving. One card in the pair has the word problem, and the other has the equation and answer. For example: The problem is "3 hexagons − 2 triangles = how many sides?" The answer is "3(6) − 2(3) = 12."

Make card decks with less pictorial support and more abstract symbols and descriptions.

Provide pictorial support—for example, one card with a picture of a triangle and three dots paired with a card with the numeral 3, or a square and four dots paired with the numeral 4.

Have students make sets with fewer cards.

Tips *from the* Trenches!

- Cutting 3 × 5-inch index cards in half makes for a nice-size deck. Provide water-soluble markers or crayons; permanent markers will soak through to the other side.

- This game doesn't have to be limited to geometry. Consider using it for numerals and their names, for the operations, for rounding, or for any other concept that needs practice and mastery. The sky's the limit!

The Details

- Level **Grades K–5**
- C–P–A **Pictorial, Abstract**
- When to Use It **Warm-Up, Conclusion, Review, Homework, Intervention / Extension**
- Time to Allow **10–20 minutes**

Plan Ahead

Player needs 28 blank cards, markers or crayons, and a rubber band or resealable plastic bag.

Connections to the **Common Core State Standards**

Content Clusters

K.G.A Identify and describe shapes (squares, circles, triangles, rectangles, hexagons, cubes, cones, cylinders, and spheres).
1.G.A, 2.G.A, 3.G.A Reason with shapes and their attributes.
4.G.A Draw and identify lines and angles, and classify shapes by properties of their lines and angles.
5.G.B Classify two-dimensional figures into categories based on their properties.

Math Practices

MP2 Reason abstractly and quantitatively.
MP7 Look for and make use of structure.

38 Tower Up

Objective

Earn cups by solving problems so you can build a tower.

Materials

Math problems, an answer key, 3-ounce cups, and a container to hold cups

Directions

Read directions to student players as needed.

1 Solve a list of math problems. Check work to be sure it is correct.

2 Get as many paper cups as you have problems and a container for the cups. Write a math problem on the outside bottom of each cup. Write the answer inside the cup. Stack all the cups.

3 Now you are ready to play. Pull a cup off the top of the stack, solve the problem, and check your answer.

4 If you get the problem correct, keep the cup. If you get it wrong, put the cup on the bottom of the stack.

5 Build a tower by stacking the cups you keep. Try to build the highest or most interesting tower you can.

6 You win when you've used all your cups to build a tower.

38 Tower Up

Why This One?

Kids, no matter their age, like to build things. This game motivates students to practice math problems so they can earn cups to build a tower. The more problems they answer correctly, the more cups they have for their towers.

 Differentiate It!

Have players use larger, more challenging numbers for their problems.

Go beyond simple arithmetic problems. Use shapes, angles, measurement conversions, fractions, and other challenging concepts.

For the youngest grades, instead of having players write 2 + 2 numerically, have them draw 2 dots + 2 dots on the outside of the cup for the problem and dots inside the cup for the answer.

So players moving at a slower pace don't get frustrated, have several cups labeled "2 free cups." If they come to one of these cups, they get to take that cup and the next one (regardless of whether they know the answer). This keeps them motivated.

 **Tips** *from the* **Trenches!**

- Have players solve the problems on paper so you can check their work before they write the answers on the cups.

- Uncoated paper cups are easiest to write on. One Pringles chip container can hold up to fifty 3-ounce cups.

- This game makes a great pre-holiday or pre-vacation "make and take." Containers can go home with students over school break for practice. When they come back, have them make new cups with more challenging problems to switch out with the old ones.

The Details

- Level **Grades K–5**
- C–P–A **Abstract**
- When to Use It
  **Warm-Up,
  Conclusion,
  Review,
  Homework,
  Intervention / Extension**
- Time to Allow
  10–15 minutes

Plan Ahead

Player needs 3-ounce paper cups, a container to hold them, a list of math problems to solve, and an answer key for checking their answers.

Connections to the
**Common Core
State Standards**

Content Clusters
K.OA.A Understand addition as putting together and adding to, and understand subtraction as taking apart and taking from.
1.OA.D Work with addition and subtraction equations.
1.OA.C, 2.OA.B Add and subtract within 20.
3.OA.C Multiply and divide within 100.
4.NBT.B Use place value understanding and properties of operations to perform multi-digit arithmetic.
5.OA.A Write and interpret numerical expressions.

Math Practices
MP5 Use appropriate tools strategically.
MP6 Attend to precision.
MP8 Look for and express regularity in repeated reasoning.

39 Group It!

Objective

Draw pictures to show multiplication as "groups of."

Materials

1 die, paper & pencil

Directions

1 Fold the paper into 8 parts, then open it to make a game board.

2 Roll the die. Draw that many open circles in the top half of one box on the game board (see illustration). For example, if you roll a 4, draw 4 circles. These are the "groups of" that you'll draw inside of.

3 Roll again. Draw that many items in each circle. For example, if you have 4 circles (or groups) from the first roll and then roll a 2, draw 2 items (such as stars, x's, or dots) inside each circle. This makes 4 groups of 2.

4 Under the picture, write a number sentence or equation—for example, "4 groups of 2 is 8" or "4 × 2 = 8."

5 Keep rolling until every box on the game board is filled.

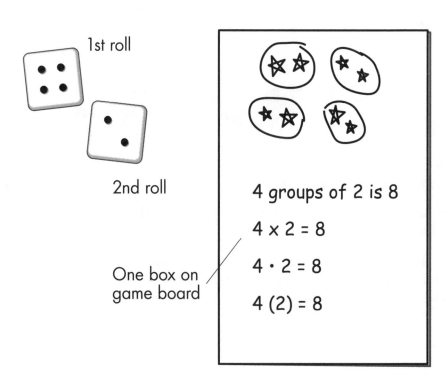

1st roll

2nd roll

One box on game board

4 groups of 2 is 8

4 x 2 = 8

4 · 2 = 8

4 (2) = 8

39 Group It!

Why This One?

The concept of "groups of" or "times as many as" is hard for students to own. Use this simple game to cement these concepts and lead kids to other concepts related to multiplication. This game is also versatile. For students who are new to multiplication, you can make the game more pictorial. For students who are ready, you can use abstract representation.

 Differentiate It!

Provide 10-sided dice for students who are ready to work with larger numbers.

Challenge players to find the sum of all the numbers rolled.

Have players use multi-digit multiplication. For example, the first roll tells how many groups; the second roll tells how many 10s to write in each group. So if a player rolls a 2 and a 5, she'd draw two large circles and then 50 dots in each. Remind players to make circles that are large enough for all those groups of 10.

Have players make groups showing values for money. For example, if the first roll is 2 and the second is 6, players first draw 2 big circles (groups), then draw 6 quarters in each circle. They then look for 4 quarters to make 1 whole dollar. You can use a similar approach for other fractions of a whole.

Allow players to use manipulatives to build each group. Then, to figure out the total number of objects, pull those manipulatives together to build groups of 10.

Let players use a multiplication chart to find multiplication facts.

 **Tips** *from the* **Trenches!**

New equipment gets students excited all over again about the same old game. When students have played this game a few times, use dice within dice to change it up. The outer (clear) die shows the number of groups, and the inner (colored) die shows the number of items in each group. Or have students fold, cut, and/or staple a sheet of paper into a little book in which they can draw the groups. Just these two little changes can make this an entirely new game in students' eyes.

The Details

- Level **Grades 2–4**
- C–P–A **Pictorial, Abstract**
- When to Use It **Lesson, Review, Homework, Intervention / Extension**
- Time to Allow **10–20 minutes**

Plan Ahead

Player needs 1 die and a sheet of plain paper.

Connections to the **Common Core State Standards**

Content Clusters

2.OA.C Work with equal groups of objects to gain foundations for multiplication.

3.OA.A Represent and solve problems involving multiplication and division.

4.OA.A Use the four operations with whole numbers to solve problems.

Math Practices

MP2 Reason abstractly and quantitatively.

MP4 Model with mathematics.

MP8 Look for and express regularity in repeated reasoning.

40 What's Left?

Objective

Use 3 numbers and 4 operations to cross off as many numbers from 1 to 20 as possible in as few rolls as possible.

Materials

Three dice, paper & pencil

Directions

1 Write the numbers 0 to 20 on a sheet of paper.

2 Roll three dice. Use the numbers rolled and the four operations (+, −, ×, ÷) to make number sentences with answers from 0 to 20. Cross off each number (answer) you use. You can make many different number sentences on the same roll, and you can use the same numbers to get more than one answer. Look at the example below.

3 When you've made all the number sentences you can, roll again. Make more number sentences using these new numbers and cross off the answers on the list.

4 Two different ways to score: go for the fewest number of rolls to cross off the whole list (up to 10 rolls), or find the total of all the numbers you didn't cross off. In both cases, lower numbers equal better scores.

Example

If you roll a 3, a 4, and a 6:

$3 + 4 = \boxed{7}$ $3 + 6 = \boxed{9}$ $4 + 6 = \boxed{10}$

$3 + 4 + 6 = \boxed{13}$ $(3 + 4) − 6 = \boxed{1}$

$(3 + 6) − 4 = \boxed{5}$

From those number sentences, you can cross off **1, 5, 7, 9, 10,** and **13**. Keep going! There are more number sentences.

$3 × 4 = \boxed{12}$ $3 × 6 = \boxed{18}$

$(3 × 4) − 6 = \boxed{6}$ $(6 × 3) − 4 = \boxed{14}$

$(4 × 6) ÷ 3 = \boxed{8}$

Cross off the new answers. You've crossed off **1, 5, 6, 7, 8, 9, 10, 12, 13, 14,** and **18** all in one roll.

40 What's Left?

Why This One?

This game makes a great "mess with the math" opportunity for practicing basic operations to the point of fluency. It's particularly useful in giving students a reasonably quiet, self-directed way to go the extra mile after they finish their regular work. And it's great for helping them understand that performing the same operations on the same numbers but in a different order can lead to different results.

 ## Differentiate It!

Have players write the equations they create using parentheses and brackets to prove each answer they came up with mentally.

Have players use 10-sided dice and a greater number range, such as 0 to 50.

Write one set of numbers for two players to share. Players take turns getting rid of numbers. The player making the last play wins. Another way to play is to have each player mark the numbers using different colors, then add the numbers they marked. The player with the greatest sum wins.

Reduce the range of numbers to 1 to 9 and use only two dice.

Ask players to build their number sentences using manipulatives to model the various ways they're utilizing the numbers.

Tips *from the* Trenches!

- For a formative assessment, ask players to record their "messings" with each roll on paper. This creates an incentive for players to persevere through multiple attempts. If you ask them to turn in their papers, you have a record of their thinking to review.

- Consider having students make a page in their math journals or notebooks with multiple lines of the numerals 1 to 20 written out, then store dice in a handy location. That way, students can play the game whenever the opportunity presents itself.

The Details
- Level **Grades 2–5**
- C–P–A **Abstract**
- When to Use It
  **Lesson,
  Review,
  Homework,
  Intervention / Extension**
- Time to Allow
  10–20 minutes

Plan Ahead

Player needs 3 dice.

 Connections to the
**Common Core
State Standards**

Content Clusters
2.NBT.B Use place value understanding and properties of operations to add and subtract.
3.OA.B Understand properties of multiplication and the relationship between multiplication and division.
4.OA.A Use the four operations with whole numbers to solve problems.
5.OA.A Write and interpret numerical expressions.

Math Practices
MP1 Make sense of problems and persevere in solving them.
MP2 Reason abstractly and quantitatively.
MP4 Model with mathematics.
MP6 Attend to precision.

PART III

Copymasters & Resources

Math Play Student Productivity Rubric

Oops (1)	So-So (2)	Great! (3)	Wow!! (4)
• off task • little or no effort • didn't help others • disrespectful • dependent • loud! • didn't use tools • no evidence	• off and on task • did the basics, but with little effort • kind of helped others • sometimes respectful • sometimes independent • high and low noise levels • used some tools • a little evidence	• mostly on task • did the basics • tried to help others • respectful most of the time • usually independent; tried to persevere • good noise level most of the time • used tools appropriately • good evidence	• on task the entire time • looked for a challenge • helped others a lot • always respectful • independent; persevered and problem-solved • used appropriate noise level • used tools strategically and appropriately • good evidence and thought about others' evidence

 Copymaster • *Math Play* • © 2015 • Crystal Springs Books

Game Reflection

Name:

_____

Game played:

_____

Partner(s):

_____

_____

What was the objective of playing the game?

_____

_____

Did you meet the objective? Yes___ No___

What did you notice while playing the game?

_____

_____

What will you try to do differently next time you play this game?

_____

_____

How would you rate your productivity while playing this game? Why?

1   2   3   4

_____

_____

Would you recommend this game to a friend?
    Yes___ No___

Why or why not? _____

_____

Game Reflection

Name:

_____

Game played:

_____

Partner(s):

_____

_____

What was the objective of playing the game?

_____

_____

Did you meet the objective? Yes___ No___

What did you notice while playing the game?

_____

_____

What will you try to do differently next time you play this game?

_____

_____

How would you rate your productivity while playing this game? Why?

1   2   3   4

_____

_____

Would you recommend this game to a friend?
    Yes___ No___

Why or why not? _____

_____

Student Progress Tracking Sheet

Student Name _____

Assessment Data _____

	STRENGTHS		GOALS	
Date	Intervention, Instruction, or Extension	Observation	Proficiency Level (1, 2, 3, 4)	Next Steps

Game 13 Math Practices Dice Roll Prompts

Roll the die before you do a math problem. Use the numbered before-task prompt to talk or write about the math. Roll again after you finish the problem. Use the after-task prompt.

Dice Roll	Before-Task Prompt	Dice Roll	After-Task Prompt
1	What's the first thing you can do to solve this problem? What strategies can you try? Why would you choose them? (MP1, MP4)	1	Is there another way to solve this problem that you can use to check your solution? Is there a different way to go about solving the problem? (MP1, MP4)
2	What question do you need to answer to solve this problem? What labels do you need in your answer statement? (MP1)	2	Were any tools essential to solving this problem? Why did you choose those tools? Could you have used others? (MP5)
3	Have you solved a problem like this before? What makes that one the same as this one? (MP7, MP8)	3	Explain how you solved an earlier problem that was like this one. How was this problem like that one? How was it different? (MP7, MP8)
4	What can you do when a problem gets hard to solve instead of giving up? (MP1)	4	What did you already know that helped you solve this problem? (MP2)
5	How will you know your answer is correct and reasonable? How can you explain and prove it? (MP3, MP6)	5	What did you do to check your answer and make sure it made sense? (MP4, MP6)
6	What do you already know how to do that will help you solve this problem? (MP2, MP7)	6	How is the way you solved the problem the same or different from the way your classmates solved it? (MP3)

Notes in parentheses list which of the 8 math practices are addressed by using each prompt.

Game 23 Stink Eye Scorecard

Follow game directions on page 70.
Write + for addition or × for multiplication in the circle for each pair of numbers rolled.

Game 1

Roll 1 _____ ◯ _____ = _____

Roll 2 _____ ◯ _____ = _____

Roll 3 _____ ◯ _____ = _____

Roll 4 _____ ◯ _____ = _____

Game 1 Total: _____

Game 2

Roll 1 _____ ◯ _____ = _____

Roll 2 _____ ◯ _____ = _____

Roll 3 _____ ◯ _____ = _____

Roll 4 _____ ◯ _____ = _____

Game 2 Total: _____

Game 3

Roll 1 _____ ◯ _____ = _____

Roll 2 _____ ◯ _____ = _____

Roll 3 _____ ◯ _____ = _____

Roll 4 _____ ◯ _____ = _____

Game 3 Total: _____

Game 4

Roll 1 _____ ◯ _____ = _____

Roll 2 _____ ◯ _____ = _____

Roll 3 _____ ◯ _____ = _____

Roll 4 _____ ◯ _____ = _____

Game 4 Total: _____

Game 5

Roll 1 _____ ◯ _____ = _____

Roll 2 _____ ◯ _____ = _____

Roll 3 _____ ◯ _____ = _____

Roll 4 _____ ◯ _____ = _____

Game 5 Total: _____

Game 6

Roll 1 _____ ◯ _____ = _____

Roll 2 _____ ◯ _____ = _____

Roll 3 _____ ◯ _____ = _____

Roll 4 _____ ◯ _____ = _____

Game 6 Total: _____

Grand Total: _____

Game 25 Ninety-Eight Card Values

King
!

Take value straight to 98.

3
←

Reverse direction of play.

4
+0

Worth 0; keep current total the same.

10
−10

Subtract 10 from current total.

Queen or Jack
+10

Add 10 to current total.

Ace
+1 or **+11**

Add 1 or add 11 (player's choice).

- Number cards not listed in the chart add their face value to the total.
- Cards 3 and 4 do *not* add to the total. They do only what's listed in the chart.
- Remember to draw a card at the end of each turn.

Game 26 Four in a Row Game Board

1 Player 1 covers two factors in the row above the game board with two paper clips, then covers the product of the factors with a playing piece.

2 Player 2 moves one paper clip to a different factor, then covers the product of the factors with a playing piece.

3 Players take turns. The first player to get four products in a row wins.

Factors: 0   1   2   3   4   5   6   7   8   9

1	2	3	4	5	6
7	8	9	10	12	14
15	16	18	20	21	24
25	27	28	30	32	35
36	40	42	45	48	49
54	56	63	64	72	81

Game 30 Par 3 Scorecard

Name: _____

	Hole 1	Hole 2	Hole 3	Hole 4	Hole 5	Hole 6	Hole 7	Hole 8	Hole 9
Target	___	___	___	___	___	___	___	___	___
3 Cards Drawn	___	___	___	___	___	___	___	___	___
More Cards Drawn (up to 5)	___	___	___	___	___	___	___	___	___
Solution									
Points	Points Hole 1	Points Hole 2	Points Hole 3	Points Hole 4	Points Hole 5	Points Hole 6	Points Hole 7	Points Hole 8	Points Hole 9

Game 31 Contigo Game Board

1	2	3	4	5	6	7	8
9	10	11	12	13	14	15	16
17	18	19	20	21	22	23	24
25	26	27	28	29	30	31	32
33	34	35	36	37	38	39	40
41	42	44	45	48	50	54	55
60	64	66	72	75	80	90	96
100	108	120	125	144	150	180	216

Resources

Books

Bender, William N., ed. 2009. *Differentiating Math Instruction: Strategies That Work for K–8 Classrooms.* 2nd ed. Thousand Oaks, CA: Corwin Press.

Burns, Marilyn. 1977. *About Teaching Mathematics: A K–8 Resource Guide.* 3rd ed. Sausalito, CA: Math Solutions Publications.

Kuhns, Catherine Jones, and Marrie Lasater. 2013. *Common Core Math in Action: Making the Standards Manageable, Meaningful & Fun.* Peterborough, NH: Crystal Springs Books.

Leinwand, Steven. 2009. *Accessible Mathematics: 10 Instructional Shifts That Raise Student Achievement.* Portsmouth, NH: Heinemann.

Marzano, Robert J., Debra J. Pickering, and Jane E. Pollock. 2001. *Classroom Instruction That Works: Research-Based Strategies for Increasing Student Achievement.* Alexandria, VA: ASCD.

Minton, Leslie, ed. 2007. *What If Your ABCs Were Your 123s? Building Connections Between Literacy and Numeracy.* Thousand Oaks, CA: Corwin Press.

Richardson, Kathy. 1999. *Developing Number Concepts, Book 2: Addition and Subtraction.* Parsippany, NJ: Dale Seymour Publications.

———. 1999. *Developing Number Concepts, Book 3: Place Value, Multiplication and Division.* Parsippany, NJ: Dale Seymour Publications.

Tate, Marcia L. 2010. *Worksheets Don't Grow Dendrites: 20 Instructional Strategies That Engage the Brain.* 2nd ed. Thousand Oaks, CA: Corwin Press.

Wall, Edward S., and Alfred S. Posamentier. 2007. *What Successful Math Teachers Do, Grades PreK–5: Research-Based Strategies for the Standards-Based Classroom.* Thousand Oaks, CA: Corwin Press.

Yeap, Ban Har, and Lorraine Walker. 2012. *Every Child Can Do Math: Deceptively Simple Activities to Develop Mathematical Thinking.* Peterborough, NH: Crystal Springs Books.

Websites

Box Cars and One-Eyed Jacks. www.boxcarsandoneeyedjacks.com. Math game books and equipment.

Common Core State Standards Initiative. www.corestandards.org.

Greg Tang Math. www.gregtangmath.com. Online math games and practice materials.

Illustrative Mathematics. www.illustrativemathematics.org. Math tasks for the Common Core State Standards.

Marcy Cook Math. http://marcycookmath.com. Books and math tasks.

Math Playground. www.mathplayground.com. Online math games and videos.

A Maths Dictionary for Kids. http://amathsdictionaryforkids.com. Definitions and printable math charts.

NCTM. Illuminations: Resources for Teaching Math. http://illuminations.nctm.org. Lessons and interactives.

Professional Development

Who Is SDE?

Staff Development for Educators is America's leading provider of professional development for PreK through Grade 12 educators. We believe that educators have the most important job in the world. That's why we're dedicated to empowering educators with sustained PD that is not only research based, innovative, and rigorous, but also practical, motivating, and fun.

We offer:

- Expertise in the most relevant cutting-edge topics and global trends facing educators today

- Access to over 300 engaging and inspiring educational experts

- A variety of PD options to fit how you learn best and that match your budget and schedule.

Educators need flexibility and variety in accessing professional development.

That's why SDE provides multiple formats to fit how you learn best.

PD Events

- Single-Topic Workshops
- Multi-Topic Workshops
- National and Regional Conferences
- Unconference Facilitation
- In-Depth Institutes
- Train-the-Trainer Institutes

Onsite PD

- Single-Topic Workshops
- Multi-Topic Workshops
- Customized Conferences
- In-Depth Institutes
- Train-the-Trainer Institutes
- Co-Teaching
- Professional Learning Communities
- Modeling/Observation
- Job Embedded Coaching

PD Resources

- Books
- Digital Resources & e-Books
- Manipulatives
- Apps
- Games

Web-Based PD

- Webinars
- Online Courses
- Flipped Workshops
- Blended Learning

Expect **Extra-**ordinary

Together let's create extraordinary classrooms.

SDE **Staff Development for EDUCATORS**

Serving the professional development needs of extraordinary educators

1-877-388-2054 | www.SDE.co